Belonging

Self and Social Discovery for Children and Adolescents

A GUIDE FOR GROUP FACILITATORS

Jayne Devencenzi & Susan Pendergast

Illustrated by Linda Lyon-Wright

D1601866

SOVEREIGNTY PRESS

Sovereignty Press
1241 Johnson Avenue, #353
San Luis Obispo, CA 93401

Manufactured in the United States of America
First printing January 1999
05 04 03 02 01 00 99   10 9 8 7 6 5 4 3 2 1

Illustrations by Linda Lyon-Wright, Walnut Creek, California
Cover design © 1999 by Lightbourne Images, Ashland, Oregon
Editing by Mark Wilson, San Rafael, California
Interior design by Zardoya Eagles, San Luis Obispo, California

---

Publisher's Cataloging-in-Publication
(Provided by Quality Books, Inc.)

Devencenzi, Jayne.
   Belonging : self and social discovery for children and adolescents : a guide for group facilitators / by Jayne Devencenzi and Susan Pendergast ; illustrated by Linda Lyon-Wright. -- 2nd ed.
       p. cm.
   Includes bibliographical references and index.
   ISBN: 0-9656025-2-4

   1. Social skills--Study and teaching--Activity programs. 2. Social learning. 3. Educational counseling. 4. Interpersonal relations in children. 5. Interpersonal relations in adolescence. I. Pendergast, Susan. II. Lyon-Wright, Linda. III. Title.

LB1139.S6D48   1999   371.4
                                                                         QBI99-18

Dedication

In Memory of Jim Sharman, who had enough faith in
our original project to give it a financial boost, and
Marianne Michels, who had enough vision to support
our fledgling efforts in the schools.

Contents

Section 1: Beginning

Section 2: The Working Stage

5 _Exploring Self_

6 _Sharing Ideas_

7   *Focusing on Feelings*

 # 8   *Making Friends*

9   *Cooperating with Others*

10   *Asserting Yourself*

13 *Resolving Conflicts*

People can be unreasonable, illogical, and self-centered.

Love them anyway.

If you do good works, people may accuse you of selfish motives.

Do good works anyway.

If you are successful, you may win false friends and true enemies.

Succeed anyway.

What you accomplish today may be forgotten tomorrow.

Accomplish anyway.

Honesty and openness may make you vulnerable.

Be honest and open anyway.

What you spend years building may be destroyed overnight.

Build anyway.

People who really want help may attack you if you help them.

Help anyway.

Offer the best that you have, and you may get hurt.

Offer your best anyway.

The world is full of conflict.

Choose peace of mind anyway.

-Anonymous

Section 1: Beginning…

Introduction

The previous edition of *Belonging* chronicled what we had learned from several years of developing emotional and social literacy programs for children in school settings in the early 1980s. Not much was happening in this arena at that time. School policies espoused the notion of educating the "whole child," but the actual content of programs supported only intellectual and physical development at best. Mental health treatment and special education programs existed for children who demonstrated serious emotional disturbances, but few—if any—supportive interventions were available for the large numbers of children whose actions were signaling less severe distress. And the notion that it was beneficial to teach all children social competencies in a developmentally sequenced manner, much as basic academic skills are taught, had little acceptance in the educational community. Still, we persevered in our attempts to address the unmet needs of children in ways that were meaningful to them, which was accomplished in great part by trusting our intuition and knowledge of child development.

During the 1990s, the necessity for the emotional support and social skills training that *Belonging* had been promoting for more than a decade was established in terms that were acceptable to the educational community. The answer to the question we have fielded over and over—"What does this have to do with children in

school?"—was provided by two easily articulated concepts: the *Triune Brain Theory* and the notion of *Resiliency*.

The Triune Brain Theory

The *Triune Brain Theory*[1] identifies three distinct parts of the human brain, describes the basic functions of each, and explains the significance of outside influences upon brain activity.

The *neocortex,* or outer portion of the brain, makes possible both spoken and written language. This part of the brain performs complex analysis, abstract reasoning, and logical and formal operational thinking. Children who are successful in school, where they spend a major portion of their waking lives, have free access to the neocortex because their basic emotional and social needs have been met.

The *limbic system,* or midsection of the brain, is responsible for emotions, recalls new information, organizes events, and acts as a person's conscience. Young people who are overwhelmed by emotional concerns at home, such as alcoholism and addiction issues or traumatic loss, "downshift" to

---

[1] The research of Paul Maclean as presented by R. and G. Caine. *Teaching and the Human Brain.* Alexandria, VA: ASCD, 1991; and L. Flart. *Human Brain, Human Learning.* New York: Longman, 1983.

the limbic system and are unable to access the neocortex, which is required for processing information and thinking at higher levels.

The *R-complex*, which consists primarily of the brain stem, directs the basic, automatic, ritualistic functions of the body that are associated with physical survival. Children who are afraid for their own safety because of family or neighborhood violence; poverty; verbal, physical, or sexual abuse; or hard-core media programming, for example, "downshift" even further and are often able to process information only at the basic, R-complex level.

Simply put, the more threatened and powerless people feel, the more difficulty they have learning anything new.

Resiliency Theory

Resiliency[2] research attempts to define the critical interventions in the lives of vulnerable children that help some "beat the odds" to become healthy and capable young people, in spite of being born into circumstances of poverty, drug addiction, abuse, and/or violence. These resilient children seem to emerge from extreme conditions because their exposure to stressful life events and threatening activities (*risk factors*) decreases; and their involvement with meaningful, life-affirming experiences (*protective factors*) increases. Caring support is put forward in this research as the first key protective factor for fostering resiliency. Two critical examples of this caring support include:

- School-based opportunities to form meaningful relationships with adults and other youth, as no other place to find social acceptance, care, and love may exist.

---

[2] E. Werner. "Protective Factors and Individual Resilience." *Handbook of Early Childhood Intervention*. NY: Cambridge University, 1991; and B. Benard. "Fostering Resiliency in Kids: Protective Factors in the Family, School and Community." Western Regional Center for Drug-Free Schools and Communities, 1991.

- A close bond with at least one person who can provide an anchor and moments of undivided attention as early in a child's life as possible.

Moving Forward

As we enter a new millennium, few people need to be convinced that children growing up in the world today need to know how to express themselves, relate to others, make informed choices, resolve conflicts, cope with stress, and adjust to change. What educators and people in helping professions need to know is how to facilitate the acquisition of the *People Skills* required to do these things well. Supported by a strong theoretical basis for our work and years of rewarding interactions with children as evidence of the efficacy of the approach, we have reworked our original efforts, reflected in the first edition of *Belonging*. This revised edition incorporates what we have learned from facilitators and children who have used our material and addresses some of the current, pressing issues of this dynamic era in human evolution.

The Revised Belonging Program

The revised edition of *Belonging* consists of two distinct sections. The first section, Chapters 1 through 4, presents a comprehensive training program for support group facilitators by giving crucial information needed to:

- understand the nature of a support group,

- learn and practice the skill requirements and responsibilities of a group facilitator,

- become familiar with the step-by-step *Belonging Group Process* format and group agreements,

- create groups with a functional composition,

- determine a focus or starting point for a given group, and

- launch, guide, and come to closure with a support group.

The second section, Chapters 5 through 13, provides the content for a comprehensive *People Skills Program* that can be used during all or part of the lifetime of a given support group. The knowledge and skills presented were developed for use in school-based support groups but also have been used effectively in many other settings, such as mental health therapy groups, substance abuse programs, and hospice grief and loss support groups. The experiences have been used as a developmentally sequenced social and emotional literacy program with large groups of individuals, as well.

The themes of each new chapter build on the last, since understanding the concepts and mastering the behaviors in early chapters make it easier to acquire those in subsequent chapters. The exercises in *Chapter 5: Exploring Self* are designed to build confidence to prepare for the communication opportunities in *Chapter 6: Sharing Ideas*. After participants practice relating their thoughts and listening to the ideas of others, the group moves toward recognizing and expressing feelings in *Chapter 7: Focusing on Feelings*.

All of the content from Chapters 5 through 7 is brought to bear in *Chapter 8: Making Friends*, which represents the change of group focus from self alone to self in relationship to others. *Chapter 9: Cooperating with Others* takes the friendship skills learned earlier and applies them to a bigger circle of people and a larger number of settings. Since many find themselves lost in group situations, *Chapter 10: Asserting Yourself* helps group members maintain an individual presence in a variety of circumstances.

The final three chapters require participants to synthesize all of the previous material, presenting the greatest challenge. Success with the content of *Chapter 11: Handling Verbal Abuse, Chapter 12: Managing Strong Feelings*, and *Chapter 13: Resolving Conflicts* requires diligent effort, but also provides the greatest opportunity for group members to use the strength of their accomplishments to diffuse the turbulence in their daily lives.

We enter the twenty-first century with our children in crisis, perhaps exhausted by the pace of our high-tech world, perhaps overwhelmed by the harsh realities constantly bombarding their senses, certainly grappling with existential issues of purpose and meaning as have all generations in the past century. We observe too many young people engaging in self-destructive behavior—suicide, early and unsafe sexual involvement, alcoholism, and drug abuse. Increasingly younger children are the perpetrators and victims of violent actions—children murdering children, date rape, hate crimes, assaults on parents and teachers, youth gang activity, etc. The revised edition of *Belonging* represents our newest, best effort to offer our children an antidote for the social condition that is their inheritance: a sense of personal and collective worth and a sense of place—of belonging.

Jayne Devencenzi
Susan Pendergast

January 1999

Assuming the Role of Facilitator

The role of a counseling support group facilitator has challenging features that distinguish it from the role of teacher or therapist. A support group is unique when compared to a school class group or a mental health therapy group, even though it is also a place for learning social skills and solving problems. Chart 1.1 outlines some distinctions among the groups.

SCHOOL • SUPPORT • THERAPY GROUP DISTINCTIONS

Chart 1.1

School Class Group	Support Group	Therapy Group
Adult teachers assume responsibility for the class group	Group members are responsible for themselves and to each other	Trained therapists take responsibility for a therapy plan
Teachers develop lesson plans and lead the learning	Group members make collective decisions and share the "point position"	Therapists actively engage clients in the therapy plan
Purpose of the program is to educate according to defined goals and objectives	Purpose of the program is to support personally and collectively defined self and social improvement	Purpose of the program is to promote healing related to specific issues
Focus is on cognitive, physical, and social development	Focus is on affective and social growth	Focus is on overall mental health
Teachers develop activities based on the skill level of the class group	Members agree upon skills to develop through group activities	Therapist provides diagnosis and treatment plan
Deals primarily with cognitive development	Highlights general self and social concerns	Deals with specific life issues

Characteristics of an Effective Facilitator

To facilitate means "to make easy or less difficult," which ironically is no easy task. Taking on the role of facilitator for the social and emotional development of a group of people is a responsibility not to be taken lightly. Anyone who considers becoming a group facilitator will benefit from time spent in self-reflection.

➡ Ask yourself: "Do I want to assume responsibility for the well-being of others? Do I have the personal qualities necessary to be an effective facilitator? Am I willing to learn the skills required to facilitate successfully?"

The characteristics described in the following passage are designed to encourage careful consideration by those who want to accept the role of facilitator.

➡ Ask yourself: "Do I know what I'm getting into?!"

A willingness to make a time commitment of at least twelve to fifteen weeks to the group experience. Making a trust connection with people and then reneging can be devastating, hindering the chances for developing future trusting relationships.

➡ Ask yourself: "Do I realistically have the time and energy to devote to this process?"

An abundant history of life experiences with children and adolescents either as a parent or in a helping profession. Strong facilitators are able to step out of the adult world and experience life through the eyes and ears of a child or young person.

➡ Ask yourself: "Am I playful? Can I think magically like a child?"

A genuine caring nature, an easy rapport with diverse groups of people, and an overall enthusiasm for life. Prospective facilitators need to consider how approachable they are and how often they offer encouragement to others.

➡ Ask yourself: "Do people speak freely around me? Do they seek my counsel and comfort?"

Emotional literacy as demonstrated by a good expressive vocabulary of feelings, strong listening skills, and a sensitivity to emotional needs. In order to promote emotional disclosure among group members, facilitators must project a sense of comfort with emotional issues and a willingness to share their own feelings.

➡ Ask yourself: "When I'm upset, am I able to verbalize my feelings? Am I able to listen reflectively and non-defensively to the feelings of others?"

Strong organizational and planning abilities paired with a flexible attitude and comfort with change. Effective facilitators bring a well-organized plan for each group session and are willing to abandon it as necessary to deal with the issues brought to the group on any given day.

➡ Ask yourself: "Am I a well-organized person? Can I 'go with the flow'?"

An acceptance of the facilitator's role as guide, not judge. Effective facilitators are nonjudgmental and help others to explore options without labeling them right/wrong or good/bad. They are able to move the group in a productive direction without being overly controlling.

➡ Ask yourself: "Am I aware of my own attitudes, biases, and prejudices? Do I value new perspectives?"

The ability to model good social skills in one's own life. When group members see their guide using the skills focused on in group, they are more apt to understand and try the new behaviors. Modeling is a powerful learning tool.

➡ Ask yourself: "Do I strive to be a positive role model? Do others follow my lead?"

Tools for Successful Facilitation

In conjunction with the characteristics discussed above, a good facilitator must possess skills that can promote growth and change for group participants. The tools which need to be honed are basic communication skills—but "basic" doesn't mean that they simply are acquired from daily living. Becoming an accomplished communicator, and hence a strong facilitator, takes commitment and practice. Mature communicators who, without apparent effort, listen and respond effectively in a wide range of settings, increase that ability over time by approaching each interaction with the intention of having a clear and meaningful exchange. The other person in any given situation is the best measure of how well someone is communicating. Strong communicators frequently "check in" with others to see if their intended message was received.

Facilitator Cue Cards

Each of the points listed in Chart 1.2, Tools for Effective Communication, is elaborated upon in the following segments. This information can be copied onto card stock, cut into separate sections, and used to cue facilitators who are learning or refining the many levels of communication skills required to guide a meaningful group experience.

Chart 1.2

Tools for Successful Facilitation

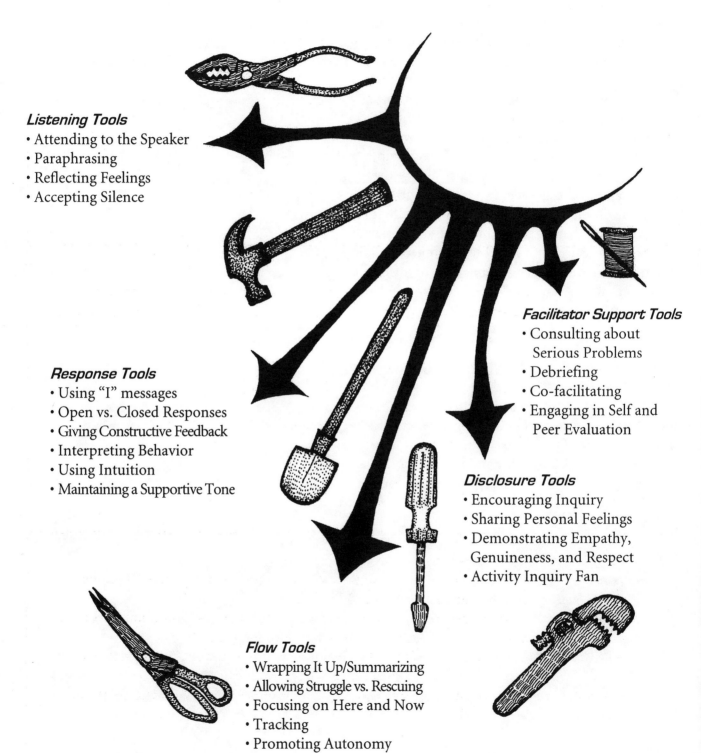

Listening Tools
• Attending to the Speaker
• Paraphrasing
• Reflecting Feelings
• Accepting Silence

Response Tools
• Using "I" messages
• Open vs. Closed Responses
• Giving Constructive Feedback
• Interpreting Behavior
• Using Intuition
• Maintaining a Supportive Tone

Facilitator Support Tools
• Consulting about Serious Problems
• Debriefing
• Co-facilitating
• Engaging in Self and Peer Evaluation

Disclosure Tools
• Encouraging Inquiry
• Sharing Personal Feelings
• Demonstrating Empathy, Genuineness, and Respect
• Activity Inquiry Fan

Flow Tools
• Wrapping It Up/Summarizing
• Allowing Struggle vs. Rescuing
• Focusing on Here and Now
• Tracking
• Promoting Autonomy

Listening Tools: Attending to the Speaker
- Pay attention verbally and nonverbally to show people that you feel that what they are saying is important. Most of the message given is nonverbal.
- Maintain eye contact when comfortable, without staring.
- Acknowledge the person speaking. *Verbal:* "Uh-huh." "M-m-m." "I see." *Nonverbal:* Nod head. Smile.
- Use supportive body language and gestures. Face the person. Lean slightly toward the person. Present an open posture.
- Remain alert and conscious of the group's process as a whole while attending to the speaker of the moment.

Listening Tools: Paraphrasing
Restate the key features of what the person said and focus upon those parts that are useful to the group's work. Use this tool to clarify information, solidify agreements, and check out a message.

- "What I heard you say is _____. Is that correct?"

- "What I think you said is _____. Is that right?"

- "We agreed that _____. Is that what you understood?"

Listening Tools: Reflecting Feelings
Bring forward the feeling(s) contained in someone's sharing. First paraphrase the content of someone's message and then suggest an associated feeling.
- "When you described your weekend spent working around the clock on homework, it sounded as if you felt frustrated (exhausted, angry with yourself, etc.)."
- "When you say that you don't care if your dad spends more time with your stepmom than he does with you, I sense some pain (sadness, anger, etc.) in your voice."
- "From what you said about never having traveled out of your neighborhood, I wonder if you might be feeling a little embarrassed (limited, afraid to try new things, etc.)."

Listening Tools: Accepting Silence

Take time to pause and reflect. Allow moments without words or activity, even if this feels awkward. Interrupting a quiet space in the group's process may signal that the facilitator is not dealing with his/her own feelings of discomfort and/or is engaged in "rescuing" behavior e.g., interfering to lessen tension rather than letting the silence unfold.

Talk about the significance of the silence only if this doesn't interrupt the flow of what comes forward after the pause. Encourage an exchange, if appropriate, with a summary statement.
- "Kevin told us about his grandmother's illness, and then we all sat very still for a minute or two."

Response Tools: Using "I" Messages

Model a response format that begins with the word "I." This demonstrates ownership of one's own thoughts and feelings and lessens the possibility of anyone feeling judged or blamed.
- "I noticed that no one offered to lend Charlie a pen when he said that he didn't bring one. I felt some tension in the circle. I wonder what that was about."

    versus
- "You didn't give Charlie a pen when he needed one. What's the matter with you guys? What if you were the person who needed one? Wouldn't you want someone to share with you?"

Statements encourage creative verbal exchange better than questions. Overuse of questioning can impair the safety level of the group by creating a threatening or confrontational tone.
- "I heard you tell how you feel about Sherry right now. I sense some real hurt in your voice."

    versus
- "Caron, I'd like to ask you why you said that you hated Sherry? I'd like to know what it is about her that you hate? I wonder how she feels about you?"

Response Tools: Open vs. Closed Responses

Respond supportively to what is actually said and felt.
- An Open Response is one that acknowledges other peoples' rights to whatever feelings are real for them in the moment. The response demonstrates that the listener accepts how the speaker is feeling as well as what is being said.
- A Closed Response denies a person's right to experience feelings and shows an overall unwillingness on the part of the listener to accept or understand the speaker's position.
- Example: "I just can't do that. I cannot get up in front of my English class and give a five minute speech."

    Closed Response: "Don't think like that, you can do it!"

    Open Response: "It's really a tough thing to do."

Response Tools: Giving Constructive Feedback

Discloses feelings related to a group member's sharing or actions and provides helpful ideas related to someone's sharing without giving advice or telling someone what s/he ought to do. Constructive feedback, always intended to be helpful, may take the form of a criticism, a compliment, or a suggestion.

- Ask permission before offering feedback. "I have some feedback for you, would you like to hear it?" or "Are you open to hearing a suggestion?"
- Keep feedback clear and concise. Include both thoughts and feelings when responding to a specific behavior.

Constructive Critical: "When you sighed and whispered to your friend, I thought that you were talking about me. I got worried."

Constructive Complimentary: "When you explained that you were sighing because you had missed breakfast and were too hungry to concentrate, I felt relieved to know that I hadn't done something wrong. I appreciate you clearing that up for me."

Response Tools: Giving Constructive Feedback (continued)

- Make realistic and respectful suggestions directly related to the experience shared. Explore many possible options for obtaining a desired change in circumstances or behavior. Honestly acknowledge situations that an individual has no power to alter and focus on those that can be improved.

Constructive Suggestion: "You shared that you feel lonely a lot at school and that you have no friends. You think it's because you're dyslexic and work with the resource teacher. Everyone here is aware that you have difficulty reading and writing. I wonder if you could eat lunch with someone from our group and meet new people through them?"

- Use an even tone of voice, especially when describing feelings about how someone is behaving in the group.

Response Tools: Interpreting Behavior/Using Intuition

Check out interpretations of possible underlying issues rather than assume to know what other people are thinking and feeling.

- "When you sighed (groaned, coughed, etc.), I thought that you were frustrated (bored, uncomfortable, etc.). I'm interested in knowing how you were feeling."
- "When you speak about your sister you use a soft (loud, gruff, etc.) tone of voice. My guess is that you feel very close to (separate from, angry with, etc.) your sister. Could you tell us about that?"
- "I notice that you are looking down at the floor a lot (wiggling a lot, watching the clock, etc.). My guess is that you are feeling anxious (agitated, bored, etc.). Am I on track?"

Response Tools: Maintaining a Supportive Tone

Remember that facilitators are helpers and guides, not teachers or leaders in a traditional sense. Present a receptive, calm, relaxed, and alert demeanor. Use facilitative language (e.g., share, relate, encourage, confront, tell the truth, trust, listen, explore, take a risk).

Participation in a support group is meant to be a worthwhile, pleasurable experience. Laughter has been studied for its healing properties, and it definitely has a place in the group. However, when humor is used to lessen tension or discomfort in the group, such "rescuing" behavior can be received as a lack of respect for the group process or as minimizing someone's sharing.

Response Tools: Maintaining a Supportive Tone (continued)

The use of touch is a controversial issue. Many facilitators are afraid to touch a group member for fear of being accused of inappropriate behavior. However, touch is not inappropriate—inappropriate touch is inappropriate. People involved in support groups need to be nurtured. Showing up, listening, and touching with words of encouragement or a caring hand on the shoulder are all important elements that help maintain a supportive atmosphere. If touch is a natural part of someone's communication style, it is useful to include thoughtful touch in the repertoire of facilitative tools. As with any communication, the test of its acceptability is the response of the other person. Always be respectful of physical boundaries, and especially so if group members have a history of abuse.

Flow Tools: Wrapping It Up/Summarizing

Reduce the important information learned and agreements made in the group in order to make sure everyone understands the same thing. For example, summarize a group activity and what everyone is to do before the next group.
- "Today we completed a feeling collage with photographs and word labels. We practiced using new words to express emotions. Before next week, we all agreed to write five sentences in our journals about our changing feelings from day to day."

✓ *Flow Tools: Allowing Struggle vs. Rescuing*

Permit the members of a group to experience some discomfort without interfering. Facilitators who try to "fix" and "make nice" indicate a lack of trust in the capabilities of the people in the group. This in turn disempowers the participants and undermines the cooperative nature of a support group.

Facilitators who find themselves wanting to protect, rescue, and/or control have a "hidden agenda" about what should be happening—unspoken expectations about what is "right" for the group.

Flow Tools: Focusing on Here and Now

Keep returning the group's focus to the present time and circumstance in order to foster hope. Avoid lapsing into lengthy storytelling about old news that no one can do anything about and that may render others "helpless and hopeless." Sharing personal history is valuable when its possible relationship to the "here and now" is explored.

- "You shared about the three animals you cared for from birth through death. I sensed a real strength in your voice when you told about the ups and downs you had together. At the end of this school year, you'll be leaving here for Middle School. That's another kind of 'happy-and-sad' story."

Flow Tools: Tracking

Note the progress that the group is making over time by periodically recapping shared experiences.

- "Since we came together as a group and agreed that 'Managing Anger' was our shared issue, we've learned how to label our feelings more clearly, remove ourselves from situations that might get us into trouble, and practice relaxation techniques in stressful circumstances."

Count down the number of sessions until the group's final meeting. Begin at least four to six weeks ahead of closure in order to lessen feelings of abandonment and betrayal that occur when the end of a group's time together is not talked about, planned for, and celebrated.

Flow Tools: Promoting Autonomy

Turn the work of the group back to its members consistently, and trust its process. For each session, bring a planned activity related to the agreed-upon focus of the group, and be able to abandon it in favor of another direction that may emerge during the process of any given meeting. Take a lesser and lesser role as the weeks go by and the maturity of the group allows. The co-facilitation feature of the Belonging Group Process demonstrates the adult facilitator's confidence in the group to manage itself from day one.

Examples of language that promotes autonomy:
- "Jeremy has been rocking in his chair for five minutes. He keeps bumping into John next to him. We have our Group Agreements posted. Does anyone want to say anything about that?"
- "Kyra, did you want to ask the group for feedback about your dilemma?"
- "Which steps in the process are you guiding today, Ned? Who co-facilitates next time?"

Disclosure Tools: Encouraging Inquiry

Encourage group members to interact with one another in order to practice new social skills and explore options that could improve a given circumstance. Facilitative statements and direct questioning promote dialogue if thoughtfully presented and interjected at opportune moments.

- *Closed Inquiry*, which consists of questions that require a "right" or a "yes/no" answer, does not result in meaningful communication among group members.
- *Open Inquiry*, when used sparingly and with the goal of encouraging further exploration of a topic, guides productive conversation.

Examples of Open Inquiry in both question and statement formats:
- Question: "How could you do this differently in the future?"
- Statement: "Mary seems stuck on this one way of handling the problem."
- Question: "How might you use this in your life?"
- Statement: "Some people start each day with a short meditation."
- Question: "What suggestions do we have for Carl and Christine?"

Disclosure Tools: Encouraging Inquiry (continued)
- Statement: "It sounds as if Carl and Christine had a particularly rough few weeks."
- Question: "How do you feel about this?"
- Statement: "Martha's fists are clenched right now, and Allison has her hands over her face."
- Question: "What thoughts did you have while this was happening?"
- Statement: "Sometimes when we witness violence our minds race."
- Question: "What were you trying to make happen?"
- Statement: "It seems that we have little control over the actions of other people."
- Question: "What do you want most from today's group?"
- Statement: "Jesse, I noticed that every time I saw you this week, you asked if group was still happening on Wednesday."

- Group members have the right to choose whether or not to answer questions and/or engage in group discussions. Inquiries made by the facilitator are not meant to coax a reluctant person into speaking.

Disclosure Tools: Sharing Personal Feelings

The support group setting is not designed to take care of the emotional needs of the adult facilitators. Use this tool only if a disclosure of the facilitator's feelings clearly will benefit the recipient. Too much sharing by the facilitator can overpower the group discussion. Facilitator disclosures that do not result in getting others to talk more about themselves are an inappropriate use of the group's time and need to be curbed.

What is shared must reveal a true feeling related to the current circumstance and not what the receiver might want to hear.
- "I was uncomfortable with my body type when I was your age. I remember how upset I often felt. I'm sorry that you're struggling and feeling sad."

Disclosure Tools: Demonstrating Empathy, Genuineness, and Respect

Set a tone of acceptance. Reinforce the notion that you are approachable and that the group is a safe place in which to expose one's strengths and weaknesses.

- *Empathy:* Strive to take another person's perspective cognitively and emotionally. Understand that if we truly could "walk in someone else's shoes," we would be saying and doing exactly the same things. Trust that all people do the best that they can, given individual life experiences and learning opportunities.

- *Genuineness:* Listen attentively to what is and isn't being said, observe what is being acted out or hidden, and make inferences carefully, without judgment, in order to demonstrate sincere concern and genuine compassion for members of the group. Respond, rather than react, to the workings of the group. Display a generous spirit and open heart. Give relevant feedback in which all elements of the message are believable (i.e., body language, tone of voice, gesture, and content are congruent).

Disclosure Tools: Demonstrating Empathy, Genuineness, and Respect (continued)

- *Respect:* Adhere to the group agreements. Display confidence in the abilities of the member who co-facilitates, as well as in the group as a whole. Model clear communication in disclosures and responses. Show up consistently and follow through with commitments that are made. Admit mistakes. Keep turning responsibility back to the group. Seize opportunities to acknowledge risks that are taken in an attempt to grow, whether or not they are successful.

Disclosure Tools: Activity Inquiry Fan

Use the generic inquiry statements and questions on pages 17 and 18 to guide discussion during and/or after any of the group activities in the Belonging Program. They are designed at increasing levels of difficulty—Knowledge, Comprehension, Application, Analysis, Synthesis, and Evaluation—to accommodate younger and more mature group composition or concrete and abstract thinking abilities, regardless of chronological age. The more interaction group members have with the information and skills focused upon in each activity, the more likely it is that they will integrate the new ideas and tools into their daily lives.

Create an Activity Inquiry Fan by copying the questions and statements onto heavy card stock, using a different color for each level (e.g., blue for the Knowledge level, red for Comprehension, orange for Application, etc.). Cut them into equal size strips and connect them in the upper left-hand corner with a metal brad. The fan can then be used by the adult facilitator and later by group members who co-facilitate during the activity phase of the group process. It helps ensure that meaningful dialogue takes place and provides group members with a constant model of how to effectively engage others in conversation.

Facilitator Support Tools: Consulting about Serious Problems

Construct an up-to-date list of available referral sources within an organization and the community. Develop a rapport with contact people for these resources. A solid network of support services might include:

- A school-based Student Study Team
- Tutorials
- Student Assistance Programs
- Special Education Personnel
- School Psychological Services
- Alcohol and Drug Abuse Interventions
- Social Services
- Child Protective Services
- Community and Private Mental Health Programs
- School and Community Nursing and Health Programs
- Big Brother and Big Sister Mentor Programs
- After-School Homework and Day Care Programs
- Law Enforcement Personnel
- Parenting Groups

Issues frequently arise within the context of a support group that are beyond the scope of the group's focus. Participation in the group may still be beneficial for the individual with more complex needs, as long as more specific interventions are also obtained. Without this additional help, the unmet needs of the group member may overwhelm others, including the facilitator, and inhibit the progress of the group. Parental involvement is essential when seeking additional help for children.

By law, any instance of suspected abuse or neglect must be reported to a local Protective Services agency by the group facilitator. Likewise, suicidal disclosures or threats to seriously harm another must be shared with the appropriate Human Services group. The procedures for such reporting need to be clearly understood prior to beginning any group.

Facilitator Support Tools: Debriefing

Create a network of colleagues engaged in group facilitation or identify a partner for the purpose of reviewing group experiences. Agree upon a regularly scheduled time to discuss areas of success and concern. Even telephone conversations can serve this function. The emotional and intellectual needs of a group facilitator are not processed within the context of the group. The facilitator is the anchor person who observes, reflects, and guides experiences for the benefit of the others involved. Whereas the work is inherently purposeful, it is also potentially draining. Time devoted to self-care and collegial support is critical to the vitality of both the facilitator and the group.

Knowledge
What did we just do in this activity?

Knowledge
What did we do in the beginning, middle, and end of this activity?

Knowledge
What are three things that we did during this activity?

Comprehension
Explain why this activity has the title that it does.

Comprehension
Tell about this activity in three sentences.

Comprehension
What do you think is the main point of this activity?

Application
How could a friend of yours take the information that we learned in this activity and use it at home, in class, at recess, at soccer practice, etc.?

Application
How could you have used this information if you had learned it last year?

Application
Think of a situation from your past. How could you handle it differently now that you have this information?

Activity Inquiry Fan

Analysis

What part of the activity was the funniest, saddest, most significant, most exciting, hardest, etc.?

Analysis

Name one thing in the activity that was about how people feel. Name one thing in the activity that was about how people act.

Analysis

What is the most important thing that we learned from this activity?

Synthesis

Think of another way to learn this information.

Synthesis

Think of a new title for this activity.

Synthesis

Make up a new activity that you could use to teach your friends what we learned.

Evaluation

How did you feel at the beginning of this activity? How did you feel at the end of it? Would you recommend this activity to people in another group?

Evaluation

Compare this activity to another one that we have done. How are they the same? How are they different?

Evaluation

How would you improve this activity?

Facilitator Support Tools: Co-facilitating

Share facilitation with another adult whenever possible. Having two adult facilitators greatly reduces the responsibility factor for each. This arrangement provides built-in support for the adults and lessens the "burn out" factor.

Co-facilitators frequently agree to focus upon different aspects of the group work:

- One may guide the group through the Group Process Steps and the other through that session's activity, therefore offering the group renewed energy throughout the session.

- One may reinforce adherence to group agreements with a particularly volatile group while the other guides the Group Process Steps.

- One may do all of the planning for a specific group while the other takes responsibility for a different group, which allows each to interact more fully with groups that hold a particular interest or challenge.

Facilitator Support Tools: Engaging in Peer and Self Evaluation

Refine and renew facilitation skills by periodically evaluating the tools that are being used, not used, or overused. The Facilitator Evaluation Guide (Form 1.3) is useful when carrying out an evaluation process.

- In situations where two adult facilitators work together, one acts as the scribe and writes down verbatim what the active facilitator is saying/doing and what happened after each utterance or action. After the group meeting, the two go over the scripted information and make note of which facilitation tools were in evidence. Goals for improvement in the use of one or two communication areas provide the focus for ongoing growth as a facilitator.

- The same evaluation process can be accomplished without a co-facilitator by video taping a session and reviewing segments or by inviting another colleague to act as scribe.

Permission must be obtained from group members before carrying out any evaluation process, because such a process requires observation of the group's activities. This invasion of the group's privacy can hinder its safety factor if the purpose for the observation is not discussed first. When trust is high, group members have little difficulty understanding and supporting the facilitator's desire to also improve.

If the idea of being "watched" by a third party or a camera is clearly threatening to a group, the process described cannot be implemented. In these instances, a facilitator may benefit from reading through the Tools for Effective Facilitation (Chart 1.2) while attempting to recall examples of how s/he is using, not using, or overusing each.

After deciding to become a group facilitator and practicing tools for successful facilitation, the facilitator next creates a group to guide through all or pieces of the Belonging Program. Chapter 2 discusses how to compose a successful group and provides a set of information-gathering tools (referral, permission, behavior checklist, and participation contract forms) to help the facilitator select people who could function well together as a support group.

Facilitator Evaluation Guide
Peer Evaluation

A. Write on a separate sheet of paper exactly what the facilitator said and did throughout the group session and what happened immediately after each action or statement. Label each facilitative behavior according to which Facilitation Tool it represents: Listening Tool, Response Tool, Flow Tool, or Disclosure Tool.

B. After the group session, review the script and note the frequency of use for each tool. Rate the effectiveness of the usage on a scale from 1–5 (1=counterproductive, 3=useful, and 5=promoted growth).

Listening Tools
1. Attending to the Speaker occurred _____ times. Effectiveness _____.
2. Paraphrasing occurred _____ times. Effectiveness _____.
3. Reflecting occurred _____ times. Effectiveness _____.
4. Accepting Silence occurred _____ times. Effectiveness _____.

Response Tools
1. "I" Statements occurred _____ times. Effectiveness _____.
2. Open Responses occurred _____ times. Effectiveness _____.
3. Constructive Feedback occurred _____ times. Effectiveness _____.
4. Interpreting Behavior occurred _____ times. Effectiveness _____.
5. Maintaining a Positive Tone occurred _____ times. Effectiveness _____.

Flow Tools
1. Wrapping It Up/Summarizing occurred _____ times. Effectiveness _____.
2. Allowing Silence occurred _____ times. Effectiveness _____.
3. Focusing on Here and Now occurred _____ times. Effectiveness _____.
4. Tracking occurred _____ times. Effectiveness _____.
5. Promoting Autonomy occurred _____ times. Effectiveness _____.

Disclosure Tools
1. Encouraging Inquiry occurred _____ times. Effectiveness _____.
2. Sharing Personal Feelings occurred _____ times. Effectiveness _____.
3. Empathy, Genuineness, and Respect occurred _____ times. Effectiveness _____.
4. Use of the Activity Inquiry Fan occurred _____ times. Effectiveness _____.

Linda Lyon-Wright 1987

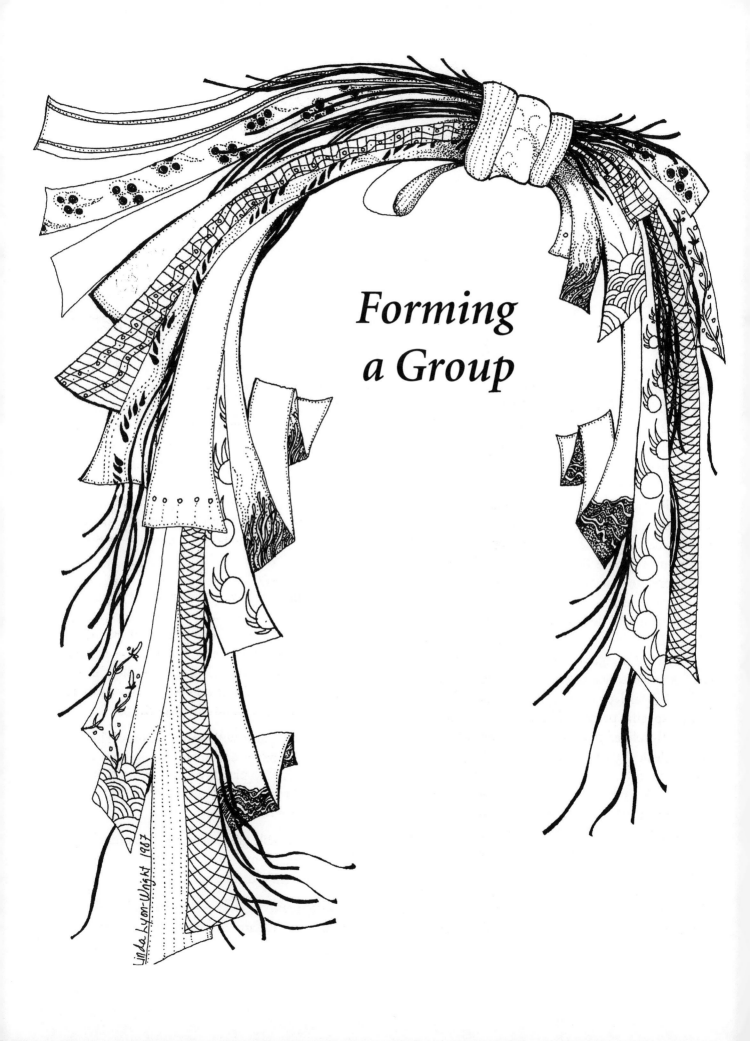

Forming
a Group

Chapter 2

Initial Referrals and Use of Forms

The Referral Form (Form 2.1), Behavior Checklist (Form 2.2), Permission Form (Form 2.3), and Group Participation Contract (Form 2.4) were designed to help facilitators group identified participants: those with common needs who could benefit from a structured social skills program and the opportunity to learn how to successfully interact in a group. As others learn of the availability of the support groups, self-referrals and parent referrals become common. The forms and letters provided are meant to be personalized to meet the needs of a particular situation. Giving the groups a friendly, descriptive name such as "Circle of Friends" makes them more inviting.

When initial referrals are received, the referring party is asked to complete the Behavior Checklist (Form 2.2), which provides more detailed information about a specific person. The items on the checklist are directly related to the content of the People Skills that are dealt with in the group. The checklist gives the group facilitator information about each individual's areas of concern, as well as areas of common concern among group members.

Including parents in the referral process through use of the Permission Form (Form 2.3) establishes a working relationship with the family, which can enhance the group member's progress. The Belonging Program recommends contact with parents, whether or not an individual state requires parental permission for participation in a counseling activity.

It is essential to obtain the consent of individual participants. Contracts such as the Group Participation Contract (Form 2.4) are sometimes useful to offer reinforcement for trying the group for several sessions before committing to membership. Potential members are simply and honestly told the purpose of the group and how it might benefit them.

Group Composition

Deciding upon the composition of any group is a formidable task. Whereas there are a few consistently relevant "tips" for accomplishing this process, often the final composition is determined by using a blend of intuition and experience. After reviewing the information obtained about a given set of potential group participants, a facilitator may choose to:

- group participants with similar issues. The group then has a common focus, which makes it easier to plan group activities. The group makes progress as a unit when everyone has a shared interest.

- create a workable group size. Five is optimal. Unless there is an adult co-facilitator, the group size should not exceed six.

- include members whose People Skill levels are within the same developmental range.

However, more socially capable individuals can serve as role models for other group members. Groups tend to rise to the level of the most capable member. Conversely, groups tend to sink to the functioning level of someone who is noticeably less capable than the rest of the group, and such a dynamic needs to be avoided.

• consider the chronological age and maturational level of potential members. Generally, a two- to three-year age range is optimal when working with children or adolescents. However, an effective grouping practice can be to combine young children with adolescents. The adolescents are "looked up to" and the young children bring a simpler, clearer way of perceiving issues that arise.

• balance the number of males and females in the group to promote a sense of inclusion and safety. Adolescents frequently work well in mixed-gender groups unless the common issues of the group are particularly gender-sensitive. Preadolescents tend to function better in single-gender groups.

• create an ethnic blend that reflects the make up of a given community, if such a mix has constructive possibilities. The ethnic composition of the group requires careful consideration, particularly in areas with gang conflict.

• consider socioeconomic factors when grouping. When the socioeconomic range is great, the difference in life experiences tends to be too diverse to make a functional group, unless the members share a common issue such as grief and loss, divorce, health problems, or substance abuse.

• keep the group limited to the original membership throughout the life of the group whenever possible. Adding new members mid-stream stirs up trust and safety issues, and causes the group to lose momentum while new members catch up to the rest of the group.

• invite another trained adult to co-facilitate the group whenever possible. If there are behavioral episodes or emotional outbursts that are disruptive to the group, the co-facilitator is able to work individually with the troubled participant(s).

Reforming a Group

At the end of a group cycle, the progress of each member is individually evaluated—with input from parents, staff members, and the specific group member—to determine the "next step" for each person. Options include:

• *Cycling Out.* The group member is ready to apply the newly learned skills in daily life, with little or no additional support.

• *Recycling.* The group member will benefit from more time in a structured support group and will join with a different set of people to launch a new group.

• *Branching Out.* The group member requires a more intensive, personal intervention such as individual school counseling or psychotherapy.

A group that is "reformed" to include some people who are totally new to the group process and others who have completed one or more cycles tends to advance through the Stages of Group Development quickly. The experienced group members have already decided that the support group is a safe place to be and, by their more-seasoned words and actions, serve as role models for the new members. Their comfort with the group process and content moves the group forward at a faster pace.

Suggestions for determining group composition were presented in this chapter. Coupled with the facilitation tools given in Chapter 1, they prepare the way for group activity to begin. In Chapter 3, five process steps and a set of suggested group agreements provide the structure for a group's journey of self and social discovery.

Referral Form

The groups I will be facilitating have the goal of learning "People Skills" (i.e., things one needs to know to get along with self and others). We will learn about:

1. Identifying our own strengths and weaknesses
2. Feelings: how and when to express them
3. Cooperating with others and making friends
4. Managing anger appropriately
5. Being assertive
6. Listening attentively
7. Recovering from mistakes and disappointments
8. Handling daily stress
9. Solving problems effectively

If you would like to recommend someone for group participation, please fill out the lower portion of this form and return it to me. Indicate "Areas of Concern" from the above list of nine People Skills.

Sincerely,

_____

Referrals:

Student_____ Areas of Concern_____

_____

Student_____ Areas of Concern_____

_____

Student_____ Areas of Concern_____

_____

Referred By_____

Date_____

Linda Lyon-Wright 1987

Behavior Checklist

Student's Name _____ Grade _____ Date _____

Name of person completing form _____

Relationship to student _____

Rate each of the listed behaviors according to how well it describes this student:
(1) not at all   (2) moderately well   (3) very well

	(1)	(2)	(3)
1. is pleased with his or her own accomplishments—ES	( )	( )	( )
2. knows his or her own strengths and weaknesses—ES	( )	( )	( )
3. expresses needs and feelings appropriately—EF	( )	( )	( )
4. is comfortable giving and receiving affection—EF	( )	( )	( )
5. is well-behaved—CO	( )	( )	( )
6. is well-liked by peers—CO	( )	( )	( )
7. thinks before speaking or acting—HV	( )	( )	( )
8. approaches new experiences confidently—AY	( )	( )	( )
9. expresses opinions well—AY	( )	( )	( )
10. accepts criticism well—SI	( )	( )	( )
11. is a good listener—SI	( )	( )	( )
12. can accept things not going his or her own way—MS	( )	( )	( )
13. adjusts well to changes—MS	( )	( )	( )
14. makes friends easily—MF	( )	( )	( )
15. resolves his or her own peer problems effectively—RC	( )	( )	( )

Please describe any other pertinent behavior:

_____

_____

_____

Key:
AY-Asserting Yourself
CO-Cooperating with Others
EF-Expressing Feelings
ES-Exploring Self

HV-Handling Verbal Abuse
MF-Making Friends
MS-Managing Strong Feelings
RC-Resolving Conflicts
SI-Sharing Ideas

Linda Lyon-Wright 1987

Permission Form

Dear _____,

_____ has been referred to a small group that I will be facilitating. The group focus is on social skills improvement. The group experiences will provide information about:

- Identifying our own strengths and weaknesses
- Feelings: how and when to express them
- Cooperating with others and making friends
- Managing anger appropriately
- Being assertive
- Listening attentively
- Recovering from mistakes and disappointments
- Handling daily stress
- Solving problems effectively

Please sign below to give permission for _____to participate in a group and return this form to me. If you have any questions, please phone me at _____.

Sincerely,

_____

I give permission for _____ to participate in a social skills group.

_____

Parent's or Guardian's signature/Date

Please share your concerns and comments:

_____

_____

_____

Linda Lyon-Wright 1987

Group Participation Contract

I agree to participate in a group for three sessions to see how I like it. Then I will decide whether or not I want to continue.

Some things I would like to learn:

1. _____

2. _____

3. _____

_____   _____
Participant's Signature   *Date*

I agree to assist you in the group. Some ways I can help:

1. _____

2. _____

3. _____

_____   _____
Facilitator's Signature   *Date*

Linda Lyon-Wright 1987

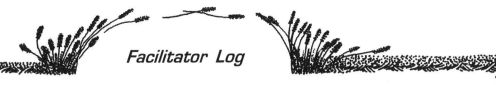

Facilitator Log

Things to remember:

_____

_____

_____

_____

_____

_____

_____

_____

_____

_____

_____

_____

_____

_____

_____

_____

_____

_____

_____

_____

_____

Learning the Process

Chapter 3

The Belonging Group Process

The Belonging Group Process provides a structure through which participants can explore "People Skills"—attitudes and actions that people need to know to appreciate and get along with themselves and others. The steps of *The Belonging Group Process* are also effective when used apart from the People Skills activities. These group process steps provide a useful structure for a wide range of counseling groups in which thematic material is presented (e.g., divorce, grief and loss, substance abuse recovery, or chronic illness support).

The Belonging Group Process has been used successfully with children eight years of age and older, as well as with adult support and parenting groups. In addition, exceptional children—those with extraordinary learning and/or emotional needs—have responded well to the process and activities.

Each group needs at least one adult facilitator. An adult co-facilitator adds to the effectiveness of the group. Ideally, the group meets forty-five minutes every week. A comfortable, quiet environment dedicated to counseling sessions is most conducive to successful group functioning. Group members sit in a circle on chairs or pillows, which helps define boundaries for group members. When space allows, two separate areas are ideal—one for group discussion and problem-solving, and another with a table for activities.

A graphic presentation of the *group process* used in *Belonging* is located on the following page (Form 3.1). Displaying this visual representation of the process in poster form is helpful when teaching and learning the format for each group meeting.

Step 1: Choose a Facilitator and Focus

Choose a Facilitator. Every group meeting begins with the selection of a facilitator (this will be the adult facilitator in the early stages of the group's life). Modeling effective leadership skills helps those who have never been in a leadership role acquire the behaviors necessary to lead. In addition, it provides those who have led through intimidation or domination of others an alternate way to maintain their position of importance without adversely effecting others. Over time, and depending upon the sophistication of group members, the facilitator determines when others are ready to serve as co-facilitators. This transition can occur when the following conditions have been fulfilled:

- The adult facilitator leads the group for at least three beginning sessions, until members feel at ease in the group.

- After these initial meetings, a volunteer from within the group shares leadership with the adult facilitator by guiding steps 2 (Share a Feeling Sentence) and 5 (Give and Receive Compliments) of the process.

Process Steps

1: Choose a Facilitator and Focus

2: Share a Feeling Sentence

"I feel _____ because _____."
"I hope to get _____ from group today."

3: Help with Problems

"I don't like it when _____.

4: Complete an Activity

5: Give and Receive Compliments

"I appreciate it when _____.

- As group members acquire more People Skills, the adult facilitator and chosen leader from the group co-lead the Focus Exercise and Step 3 (Help with Problems) in the process.

- When group time is used for direct teaching and practicing of a new People Skill, implement Step 4 (Complete an Activity) of the process. The adult retains the facilitator role.

Focus. Once the question, "Who's going to be the facilitator?" has been successfully answered, the adult's task is to help everyone turn attention toward the workings of the group and away from outside distractions. A short, simple, calming exercise serves to quiet the minds and bodies of the group members. A sample Focus Exercise follows:

Getting Present—The facilitator asks participants to close their eyes and then says: "It's time to relax our bodies and focus our minds. Begin by tightening the muscles in your face. Hold it while I count to three. One, two, three. Now release the tension in your face and move to your neck. Tighten the muscles in your neck while I count to three. One, two, three. Release. Move down to your shoulders and shrug your shoulders. Hold them up tightly to my count of three. One, two, three. Next focus on your arms. Using both arms, make a muscle and tighten your fists while I count to three. One, two, three. Relax your arms and tighten your stomach. Hold. One, two, three. Think about your legs. Tighten the muscles in your legs while I count to three. One, two, three. Relax. Finally, turn attention to your feet. Curl your toes and hold the tension to the count of three. One, two, three. Rest your feet on the ground and take one really deep breath. Breathe in deeply and exhale. Open your eyes. We're ready to begin."

Step 2: Share a Feeling Sentence

The first task of the chosen facilitator is to ask all group members, moving from person to person around the circle, how they are feeling. One

purpose of this step is to focus members' attention on each other. Another purpose is to identify any negative feelings brought to the group and determine the problems related to those feelings.

The structure used for stating feelings is modeled by the facilitator until its use is automatic:
"Today I feel _____ because _____.
And what I hope to get from group today is _____."
or
"Right now I feel_____because _____. I hope to get _____ from our group today."

The facilitator has the additional task of being a reflective listener and restating the essence of what each group member says, without repeating verbatim. For example:
"It sounds as if you feel_____ because_____."
or
"I heard you say that you feel_____ because _____."

As the group begins, all words and reasons are acceptable, as long as they fill the blanks in the model sentence. Initially, the leader makes suggestions only if someone says, "I feel like _____" instead of using a feeling word. For example, "Right now I feel like cutting class because I can't do the work."

In this case, the facilitator acts as a guide by giving several feeling words from which to choose and by asking the member to restate the feeling sentence. To complete the example given, the facilitator says, "Do you think you feel sad, angry, or confused?"

After a word choice is made, the leader asks the member to state, "Right now I feel angry because I can't keep up in that class."

Group members who are reluctant to share feelings out loud, either because they lack a vocabulary for emotions or they are resisting active participation in the group, may benefit from the use of the Feeling Cue Cards on Form 3.2. Each group member is given a strip of pictures, which allows

Feelings Cue Cards

Copy this page and cut into strips of four pictures each. Make enough strips for each group member to have one.

them to point to their current feeling state or fold the paper to cover all but their chosen emotion. The facilitator then verbalizes the emotion they indicated. The goal is to transition these group members from the use of the pictures to verbal sharing of emotions when they are ready.

Over time, a great deal of energy is spent learning to label and disclose feelings, as this is an essential People Skill. These opening feeling statements become clearer and more specific with practice. The connections between events, thoughts, and resulting feelings become more apparent.

Now that the group is aware of everyone's presence and feeling state, the experience moves in one of two directions:

> • Step 3: Help with Problems
> or
> • Step 4: Complete an Activity

Step 3: Help With Problems

The facilitator must be prepared to direct activities centering on a specific People Skill and equally prepared to abandon the activity in favor of working through a problem with a group member. Many times both problem solving and skills work happen in the same session. The more People Skills are practiced, the more realistic the problem solving will become.

When members bring problems to the group, they are responsible for stating the problem to the rest of the group. Before the group has practiced the problem-solving model presented in Chapter 13, the adult facilitator guides members toward focusing on behaviors, rather than people. For example: If someone says,

"I don't like him."

the leader asks the member to restate the problem:

"I don't like it when _____."

The individual sharing the problem asks group members for help with possible solutions. The adult facilitator assists by asking questions such as:

"What's the problem? Tell us more."

"What have you tried to do about it already? Is it helping?"

Step 4: Complete an Activity

All of the activities in *Belonging* are designed to teach People Skills. Each chapter focuses on a different People Skill in ascending order of difficulty or complexity, i.e. the skill level mastered in each chapter provides a foundation for the next series of activities. In addition, some activities have Level I and Level II options to accommodate a younger/less sophisticated and older/more skilled group composition. All activities have Awareness, Practice, and Transfer components to offer opportunities for new behaviors to be clearly understood within the safety of the group setting and then tried in the "real world."

During the initial phase of a group's development, the trust-building/group cohesion activities presented in Chapter 4 are good choices. Once the group matures and enters the Working Stage, the facilitator's ability to select activities that effectively address the needs of group participants becomes paramount. One approach is to take the group through each People Skill in sequence from Chapter 5 through Chapter 13. Another possibility is to focus on People Skills deficits and conduct activities from a particular section of the program only. The information gained from the checklists and surveys in Chapter 2 is helpful in determining a starting point.

The Activity Inquiry Fan presented in Chapter 1 can to be used in conjunction with each session's activity. These guiding questions and statements promote a deepening understanding and mastery of the information and People Skills presented.

Step 5: Give and Receive Compliments

The ability to give and receive compliments with ease is characteristic of an assertive person. When learning the process, group members are asked to compliment or say something positive about someone in the group. Sample structures for giving compliments are:

"(name), I like it when _____."
"(name), I appreciate it when _____."
"(name), I admire you for _____."
"(name), I think you _____."
"(name), thanks for _____."

The facilitator especially needs to encourage compliments related to something someone said or did in group, as opposed to how someone looks or general statements about their character. For example: "Tony, I like your shirt." or "Angela, I think you are nice." are redirected by the facilitator: "Can you also think of something special they did or said in group today?" Statements such as: "Tony, I like the way you looked at me when you had something to say." or "Angela, I appreciated your suggestion about my problem." are more personal.

Compliments given to individuals tend to be more powerful than those offered to the entire group. For example: "Zoey, thank you for cheering me up today." has more impact on an individual than "You all were nice to me today."

Often, receiving a compliment is more difficult than giving one. A good practice is to identify to whom the compliment is given before saying it. For example, "Shirlee, I have a compliment for you, OK?" This gives the receiver a chance to refuse, if accepting a compliment is uncomfortable.

Group members learn that saying a simple "thank you" and nothing more is a clear, powerful way to show that a compliment has been received and appreciated. Members are encouraged to let a compliment "soak in" before giving one to someone else.

Acknowledging personal growth by delivering a "self-compliment" is a valuable method for building healthy self-esteem among group members. For example: "I'd like to acknowledge myself for being assertive in group today. I said what I didn't like about the activity that we did."

Group Agreements

While learning the process, emphasis is placed upon following the Group Agreements. Behavioral guidelines are most effective when the group has ownership of them. The Agreements created by a given group are posted at each group meeting for easy reference and to provide reminders of mutually agreed upon behavior expectations.

Brainstorming expectations is one of the group's first tasks. The Group Agreements presented here (see form 3.3) are put forward by the facilitator as part of this brainstorming process. The suggested agreements are written in Level I and Level II formats. Level I is presented in concrete language with pictorial clues for younger children or people with limited social skills. Level II is stated in broader terms for more advanced, older group participants.

Group Agreements – Level I
• Pay attention. Look at the speaker.
• Stay in your own space.
• Wait for your turn to speak.
• Be supportive. No put-downs.
• Pass if you choose.
• Participate in group activities.
• Be respectful and confidential.

Group Agreements – Level II
• Listen attentively and carefully.
• Respond supportively.
• Pass if you choose.
• Participate in group activities.
• Be respectful and confidential.

All groups require work learning to put Group Agreements into practice, some more than others. Skilled facilitators listen for the message behind acting-out and withdrawn behaviors, which may take the form of teasing, provoking, swearing, refusing to participate, yawning, expressing boredom, and/or withdrawing.

People typically behave in certain ways—either consciously or unconsciously—for specific reasons, to get particular needs met. Chart 3.4, found on page 38, lists unmet needs and the behaviors, thoughts, and feelings associated with them. It also represents some of the issues that motivate dysfunctional behavior and suggests basic strategies for facilitator interventions.

Throughout the life span of a group, the Group Agreements Chart is referred to whenever a behavioral issue occurs. Acting as a guide and not as the-person-in-charge, the facilitator turns the issue at hand back to the group by saying something like: "Does anyone else mind that George always passes?" or "Is anyone else bothered by the noise that Karen is making?"

Group Agreements Level I

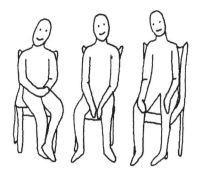

Participate in group activities.

**Pay attention.
Look at the speaker.**

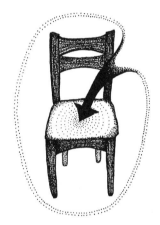

**Stay in
your own space.**

Pass if you choose.

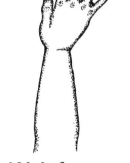

**Wait for your
turn to speak.**

**Be supportive.
No put-downs.**

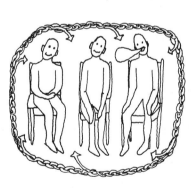

**Be respectful and
confidential.**

Chart 3.4

Unmet Need	Behaviors Expressed	Mistaken Thinking	Underlying Feelings	Facilitator Task
Attention and recognition	Showing off, pestering, interrupting the group	"I am important and belong only if you pay attention to me."	Left-out, rejected, forgotten	Acknowledge all contributions made to the group. Offer many opportunities to express themselves.
A sense of power and significance	Arguing, opposing, refusing to participate in group	"I have to be in charge or I don't count."	Anxious, insignificant, out of control	Avoid power struggles by offering choices. Provide many leadership opportunities.
Revenge and retribution	Defying, fighting, putting others down in group	"You hurt me, so I'm going to hurt you back."	Threatened, enraged, cheated	Build trust by listening reflectively and nondefensively. Promote encouragement and support from within the group.
A sense of self-worth and hope	Giving up, withdrawing, self-deprecating talk, passing in group	"I won't do it right, so why try?"	Hopeless, alone, inferior	Offer small steps to ensure success and recognize even partial attempts. Demonstrate faith in their abilities and avoid over-protection.

The facilitator helps group members define what they don't like, how they feel about it, and what would make the situation better. For example:

"George, I don't like it that you always pass when it's your turn."

"I feel frustrated because you don't participate and let us know your ideas."

"Instead of passing, I'd appreciate it if you would share with us at least once or twice during group."

The role of facilitator was clarified in Chapter 1, guidelines for determining group composition were explained in Chapter 2, and the steps of the Belonging Group Process have been outlined in this chapter. The knowledge and skill gained from these chapters can now be applied to a real group. The next chapter considers the Stages of Group Development and necessary confidentiality and child abuse reporting practices in preparation for the first meeting of a newly formed group. A series of getting-acquainted and trust-building activities help the fledgling group in its Opening Stage of development.

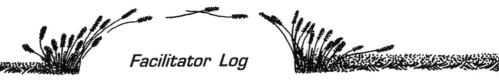

Facilitator Log

Things to remember:

_____

_____

_____

_____

_____

_____

_____

_____

_____

_____

_____

_____

_____

_____

_____

_____

_____

_____

_____

_____

_____

Launching
a Group

Chapter 4

Stages of Group Development

The life span of a group consists of three growth phases—Opening, Working, and Closing. The completion of these stages of group development naturally determines the length of a particular group experience. The success of a group and the progress made by group members depends in part upon the facilitator's ability to choose activities that are appropriate for the group's developmental level at that time.

The People Skills activities in *Belonging* are developmentally sequenced. The skills practiced in each section of the program are increasingly complex in nature and build upon those previously learned. In the Opening Stage of group development, the material in Exploring Self, Sharing Ideas, and Focusing on Feelings provides the best forum for the group's tasks and issues. As groups mature into the Working Stage of group development, the activities in Making Friends, Cooperating with Others, and Asserting Yourself challenge group members to push limits and take risks. In the latter portion of the Working Stage, and as the group enters the Closing Stage of group development, facilitators draw upon the experiences from the most complex People Skills: Handling Verbal Abuse, Managing Strong Feelings, and Resolving Conflicts.

Skilled facilitators learn to listen and watch for the signals that indicate that the group is moving from one phase of development to the next. They guide, but do not intrude upon, the natural evolution of the group and allow group members to move through these stages of development at their own pace.

Opening Stage: What Am I Doing Here?!

Group Tasks:
- Develop Trust Relationships
- Build a Cohesive Group

Facilitator Functions:
- Facilitate the creation of Group Agreements
- Promote the active use of the Group Agreements
- Guide members through the structured Belonging Process
- Plan and Implement activities
- Encourage participation without pushing
- Notice when the group moves to the next level

Look and Listen for:
- Group members freely talking about themselves, expressing feelings, and sharing hopes or expectations.

Typical Group Issues:
- Safety: How is confidentiality handled? What and how much is okay to share?
- Inclusion: What do I have in common with these folks? Do I want to fit in here? Will I fit in?

Working Stage: We Can Do This, Can't We?!

Group Tasks:

- Disclose more. Take more risks
- Become more assertive and responsible
- Understand more about the connection between thoughts, feelings, and actions
- Try out new ways of thinking and behaving
- Begin to effectively resolve conflict
- Practice coming to a consensus
- Move toward autonomy

Facilitator Functions:

- Maintain the Group Agreements, especially around confidentiality
- Allow the group to struggle
- Consistently encourage group participation
- Facilitate the use of the People Skills being learned
- Share facilitation tasks with group members
- Consult with colleagues for support and growth as a facilitator
- Notice when the group moves to the next level

Look and Listen for:

- Group members feeling comfortable enough to express diverse opinions, share suggestions with one another, and assume a co-facilitation role.

Typical Group Issues:

- Pushing Limits: How can I get my needs met?
- Challenging Authority: How can we make this group our own?

Closing Stage: I'm Ready to Move On, Aren't I?!

Group Tasks:

- Integrate the group experiences
- Say good-bye to the group
- Learn other avenues of support

Facilitator Functions:

- Review People Skills practiced to assist group members in applying them to their daily lives
- Provide ample time for members to share what the group experience has meant to them

- Model the communication skill of saying "good-bye"
- Explore other support systems with group members
- Consult with specific group members and concerned adults (parent, teacher, therapist, etc.) when ongoing support appears to be needed

Look and Listen for:

- Group members expressing thoughts and feelings about saying good-bye and applying the skills learned outside of the group setting.

or

- Group members demonstrating excessive distress over the loss of group support and reverting to old behavior patterns.

Typical Group Issues:

- Reflection: "What have I really gotten from this group? What have I given to it?"
- Readiness: "Am I ready to say good-bye?"

Confidentiality

Group facilitators must have a thorough working knowledge of the laws, policies, and ethical standards relating to confidentiality, as defined by the organization within which they work. In the absence of such guidelines, counseling facilitators should consult the American School Counselors Association (ASCA) Ethical Standards for School Counselors, which was revised in 1992.

Since active participation and self-disclosure is required for a group to move through the Stages of Group Development, it is essential to have an agreement regarding the privacy of privileged information. The agreement among group members relating to the maintenance of confidentiality may require frequent review and clarification.

Sample Explanation: "What is said and done in this room remains in this room. You may choose to share what you said or did but not if it reveals the words or actions of another member." (Ask: "How do you think this will make the group work better?")

"There are other significant people in all of our lives, such as parents, teachers, doctors, and therapists, who want to help us solve problems or reach goals. They may want to know the general information we are focusing on in our group meetings." (Ask: "Is there anyone who has a problem with this? If so, I will inform you and work with you before speaking with anyone else.")

"It's one of my jobs as a facilitator to make sure that you are safe. If you indicate that you or someone else is in danger, I must and will seek help." (Ask: "Can you name other people who will be of help in such situations?")

"If I think that you or someone else is in danger of being hurt, I will talk to you before seeking other help. I may need to contact someone from Child Protective Services or law enforcement. I will continue to help and support you, as well as keep you informed." (Ask: "How can other group members support someone who may be in a difficult life situation?")

Modeling the Process

In the beginning of a group's life, a primary task for the adult facilitator(s) is to actively model the five Group Process Steps while guiding members through inclusion or get-acquainted exercises. As the group meeting moves through these five parts, the facilitator identifies each step along the way, demonstrates the communication format for each one, and assists members as they attempt to communicate within that structure. Frequent reference is made to the visual cues provided on the Group Process Steps poster (Form 3.1). More detailed information on the five Process Steps is provided in Chapter 3.

Opening, Energizing, and Closing Activities

The last part of this chapter includes a variety of Opening and Closing Stage activities, as well as Energizing activities to use if and when the vitality of a group wanes. There are more activities than will be needed to launch, energize, or close any group. Still, facilitators are cautioned not to move too quickly from the non-threatening Opening Stage activities into the People Skills activities that are presented in chapters 5-13. Likewise, facilitators are advised to allow ample time for a series of Closing Stage activities to ensure that the ending of the group experience is memorable.

Opening Stage Activities

By participating in the following introductory activities, members may, and hopefully will:

(1) find the group a safe and fun place to be,

(2) see themselves as a valued member of the group, and

(3) begin to trust other group participants enough to make some simple, self-disclosing statements.

The facilitator selects activities appropriate for a given group and returns to them as a source of renewed energy when needed.

Brainstorming Group Agreements
Opening Activity

This activity may not be effective with younger children, in which case the facilitator posts the suggested group agreements from *Belonging*, as listed in Chapter 3 (Form 3.2), and explains that these are designed to help everyone get along better and feel safe in the group. Reference is made to the agreements whenever necessary to maintain the integrity of the group.

Objective:

Group members will anonymously state what they will contribute to the group, what they hope to gain from the group, and anything that could keep those things from happening to promote safety and trust.

Materials:

Slips of paper or 3x5 cards, pencils, basket, chart paper, marking pens

Procedure:

The facilitator begins by telling group members, "The end product of the activity is to have a list of agreements for how we want to relate to each other in order to make the group a safe and productive place for everyone."

Group members are then given a piece of paper or 3x5 card and instructed not to put their names on these. They are asked to complete the following sentence on one side of the card:

"What I have to contribute to the group is_____."

On the other side of the paper, each person writes an ending to the following sentence:

"What I hope to gain from the group is_____."

Members place their cards in a basket passed around by the facilitator, who then reads each card in turn and asks:

"Can you think of anything that could happen in this group that would keep this person from being able to contribute or gain these things?"

The facilitator or another group member records on chart paper comments made by others in response to this question. Typical responses are:

"Not being able to trust others, because someone gossips about what we discuss."

"Not feeling comfortable here, because people fight or call me names."

"Not feeling heard, because someone doesn't listen and interrupts a lot."

"Not being sure if anyone here likes me."

The facilitator may need to pose guiding questions to get the discussion focused on behaviors that would keep someone from having a meaningful group experience. A sample question would be "Could this person make the new friends that she wants if someone makes fun of the things she says in group?"

Group members identify similar responses and group these together. The facilitator then guides a discussion about what sort of agreements the group could make that would take care of some of these potential problem behaviors. The sample Group Agreements from Chapter 3 are used by the facilitator as a measure of what the group needs to create in order to ensure a safe, learning environment for everyone. Any set of Group Agreements must include one about confidentiality. The final list of Group Agreements is written to be posted at each subsequent group meeting. A powerful means of securing everyone's commitment to the Group Agreements is to have each member sign the list that they as a group created.

Inquiry:

The facilitator guides the group sharing of information by adapting the questions and statements in the Activity Inquiry Fan to the content of this experience.

Samples:

What was the purpose of this activity?

What might happen in a group that didn't have a list of Group Agreements?

What do you think is the most important agreement we wrote?

Name Game
Opening Activity

Objective:
Group members will volunteer to participate in a nonthreatening activity to get acquainted.

Materials:
None

Procedure:
The facilitator begins by telling group members that they will be playing a name game. No specific directions are given. Members listen to the facilitator's example and then volunteer to participate. First is the facilitator's own name, followed by a mode of transportation, and a place. Each item stated starts with the first letter in the person's first name. For example: "My name is Fred. I drive a Ferrari. I'm from France."

Inquiry:
The facilitator guides the group sharing of information by adapting the questions and statements in the Activity Inquiry Fan to the content of this experience.

Samples:
What is another way that we could learn each other's names?
Can you recall the three things that one other person said (name, mode of transportation, place)?
How did it feel to participate in this game?

Treasure Hunt
Opening Activity

Objective:

Group members will interact to gain knowledge about each other in order to encourage the disclosure of personal information.

Materials:

"Treasure Hunt" sheet (Experiences 4.1 and 4.2), pencils

Procedure:

Members are given a "Treasure Hunt" sheet (Experience 4.1 or 4.2). They are asked to find others who fit the descriptions on the worksheet. When members find people who fit an item, those persons sign their names in the appropriate spaces. More than one person may sign the same item. Members may sign their own sheets once. After completing the Treasure Hunt, members share what they learned about each other.

Inquiry:

The facilitator guides the group sharing of information by adapting the questions and statements in the Activity Inquiry Fan to the content of this experience.

Samples:

What did you learn about someone that you didn't know before?
How did it feel to ask other people for information about themselves?
How did it feel to have people ask you for information?
Which descriptions on the Treasure Hunt sheet fit you, if any?

Treasure Hunt #1

Find someone who:

1. knows how to ride a horse. _____

2. doesn't have any brothers. _____

3. wears the same size shoe as you do. _____

4. talks on the phone every day. _____

5. has flown in an airplane. _____

6. has an older sister. _____

7. has a birthday in the same month as you. _____

8. has a living great-grandparent. _____

9. knows how to make an omelet. _____

10. has been to a foreign country. _____

Treasure Hunt #2

Find someone who:

1. is an only child. _____

2. gets 6–8 hours of sleep daily. _____

3. has a collection of some kind. _____

4. has volunteered to help someone. _____

5. believes in fairy tales. _____

6. likes to eat Italian food. _____

7. has experienced divorce. _____

8. has been backpacking. _____

9. loves to read. _____

10. has the same color eyes as you. _____

Have You Ever?

Opening Activity

Objective:

Group members will acknowledge things they have in common with each other to promote inclusion.

Materials:

None

Procedure:

The facilitator instructs group members to raise their hands if they've ever experienced any of the events described. The facilitator says, "Have you ever… "

- been in a parade?
- had a nightmare?
- been to a costume party?
- seen a whale in the ocean?
- won an award?
- been bitten by a dog?
- eaten sushi?
- been in a performance?
- seen a car accident?
- seen a sunset over the ocean?
- seen a tornado?
- experienced an earthquake?
- stolen anything from a store?
- gossiped about a friend?
- started a rumor?
- cheated on a school assignment or test?
- blamed someone else for something you did?

The facilitator invites group members to make up other scenarios after everyone is comfortable and actively participating in the sharing.

Inquiry:

The facilitator guides the group sharing of information by adapting the questions and statements in the Activity Inquiry Fan to the content of this experience.

Samples:

How did you feel about sharing personal information about yourself?

Who else has had one or more of the same life experiences as you?

How does it feel to know that people in our group have things in common?

Guess Who?
Opening Activity

Objective:

Group members will share one item of personal information with the rest of the group to demonstrate increasing levels of trust within the group.

Materials:

One 3x5 card for each group member, pencils

Procedure:

Group members write something about themselves that no one else knows (and that they wouldn't mind making public information) on a 3x5 card. They do not put their names on the cards. The facilitator gives some suggestions such as: a famous person in the family, a place they've lived before, animals they have at home, illnesses they've had, etc. After all of the cards are completed, members drop them into a bag. Everyone takes a turn selecting a card from the bag and reading it aloud. If the activity is done with young children or those having learning problems, it may be necessary for the facilitator to read the cards. Everyone guesses who belongs to which piece of information. The facilitator asks questions to encourage the sharing of ideas and feelings.

Inquiry:

The facilitator guides the group sharing of information by adapting the questions and statements in the Activity Inquiry Fan to the content of this experience.

Samples:

What part of this activity was the easiest? The hardest?
What did you learn about two other people?
What was the point of this activity?

The Web
Opening Activity

Objective:
Members will share information about themselves with the group and be able to remember one item someone else shared to develop a sense of connection among group members.

Materials:
A ball of yarn

Procedure:
Group members sit on the floor in a circle. The facilitator holds onto the end of the yarn and shares something about herself using the suggested topics listed below. The ball of yarn is then rolled to another group member, who in turn holds onto the yarn and shares something about himself. As the yarn moves from person to person, a web is formed. Members get a visual picture of how they are joined together as a group. Members are asked to try to remember what someone else said.

Suggested topics, moving from nonthreatening to self-disclosing, include:
1. If you could be an animal, what would it be?
2. What is something you do well?
3. What do you enjoy doing in your spare time?
4. What is your favorite color, song, place, food, etc.?
5. Who is someone important to you? Why?
6. What is something you wish for or hope to do?

Inquiry:
The facilitator guides the group sharing of information by adapting the questions and statements in the Activity Inquiry Fan to the content of this experience.

Samples:
What was this activity like for you?

Tell about something that you learned.

When you looked at our finished web, what did it tell you about being in a group in which everyone participates?

Energizing Activities

At times it becomes apparent that a group is "bogged down"—participants don't appear to have much enthusiasm for the group experience or the group energy seems fragmented and unfocused. A wise facilitator will shift from the planned agenda and introduce one or more of the following Energizing Activities to revitalize the group.

In My Head
Energizing Activity

Objective:

Members will create a silhouette and list of personal traits and preferences to share to reenergize a sluggish group.

Materials:

Sheets of paper large enough to draw a life-size facial silhouette and marking pens

Procedure:

The facilitator passes out paper and pens and asks members to draw a life-size profile of their face. Inside of the empty silhouette, members write or draw responses to the following:
- daydreams that they have
- things that worry them
- happy times that they remember
- people and places that are important to them
- pastimes that they enjoy

When everyone is finished, group members hold their silhouettes in front of them and walk around the room observing what others have written or drawn. When members find an item on another person's silhouette that they also have on theirs, each person circles it with a marker and resumes walking and marking shared responses as time allows (3–5 minutes.) Shared items are tallied and discussed.

Inquiry:

The facilitator guides the group sharing of information by adapting the questions and statements in the Activity Inquiry Fan to the content of this experience.

Samples:

How did it feel to have others know what goes on in your head?

Did anybody write or draw any of the same things that you did? How did that feel?

What else would you like to have people tell about on their silhouette?

Line Up!
Energizing Activity

Objective:
Group members will work collectively to organize themselves according to various parameters to lighten the mood of a tired group.

Materials:
None

Procedure:
The facilitator informs group members that the activity will be accomplished silently, using only nonverbal cues. Members are asked to line up according to each of the following descriptors, which requires them to constantly move and reorganize without talking.
1) Alphabetically by first name then by last name
2) Size of their feet from largest to smallest
3) Height from smallest to largest and then vice-versa
4) Date of birth—January through December
5) Last four digits of their Social Security number
6) Hair color from lightest to darkest, then from shortest to longest
7) Age from oldest to youngest
8) Dirtiest to cleanest hands

Inquiry:
The facilitator guides the group sharing of information by adapting the questions and statements in the Activity Inquiry Fan to the content of this experience.

Samples:
What would have been different about this activity if we had been able to talk?
What were the easiest "line-ups"? The hardest?
Think of another way to line up.

Side by Side
Energizing Activity

Objective:

Group members will discover similarities and differences between themselves and one other group participant in order to take a fresh look at group members.

Materials:

Construction paper (11x17) and marking pens

Procedure:

The facilitator asks group members to pair up with someone whom they don't know well. The pairs identify five ways in which they are alike and five ways that they are different. They record these on a sheet of paper that is shared between them. On the reverse side of the paper, the teams draw two pictures. On one-half of the paper, one person draws an illustration of how the two are alike while the other person illustrates how they are different. Each pair presents its shared discoveries to the rest of the group.

Inquiry:

The facilitator guides the group sharing of information by adapting the questions and statements in the Activity Inquiry Fan to the content of this experience.

Samples:

What could be another title for this activity?
What are two discoveries that you and your partner made about each other?
Think of someone else with whom you could do this activity. Why did you choose this person?

Toss It
Energizing Activity

Objective:
Group members will repeat a pattern ball toss to successfully complete a cooperative game in order to revitalize and restore group focus.

Materials:
Three lightweight balls (suggest foam balls approximately 4" in diameter)

Procedure:
Step 1: Group members, including the facilitator, stand in a circle. The facilitator tosses one of the balls to another member while calling his or her name. That person throws the ball to another participant after calling out his or her name. This process continues until everyone receives the ball. The last person tosses the ball back to the facilitator who restarts the pattern by saying the name of the person to whom it was first thrown and each subsequent person tosses the ball to the same person as before after calling out his or her name.

Step 2: After the group has successfully mastered the toss pattern with one ball in play, the facilitator adds a second ball. The second ball is tossed to the same pattern of people so that two balls are moving around the group at the same time. A third ball is introduced if the group achieves mastery with the two balls.

Step 3: After group members have succeeded in repeating the cooperative pattern with three balls for several rounds, the facilitator removes one ball at a time as it is returned, until all three have been removed and the activity comes to an end.

Inquiry:
The facilitator guides the group sharing of information by adapting the questions and statements in the Activity Inquiry Fan to the content of this experience.

Samples:
How did you feel as more balls were added to the game?
What are some reasons you can think of for doing an energizing activity like this?
On a scale of 1–5 (1 being "poor" and 5 being "great"), how do you think the group did?

Maybe This/Maybe That
Energizing Activity

Objective:

Group members will suspend their beliefs about what a common object is, imagine what it could be, and share their ideas around the group to bring a renewed sense of possibility to the group.

Materials:

Common objects such as a ball, a pencil, a cup, a sheet of paper, any small object that is close at hand

Procedure:

The facilitator holds an object, such as a pencil, and describes something else it could be. For example, "I think this could be a fairy's telephone pole." The object is passed to each person around the circle. Each describes another possibility for the item. Other items are introduced as time and the interest of the group allow.

Inquiry:

The facilitator guides the group sharing of information by adapting the questions and statements in the Activity Inquiry Fan to the content of this experience.

Samples:
Which description did you like the best?
What other objects could be used in this activity?
What did you learn by doing this activity?

Closing Stage Activities

As a group reaches the Closing Stage, it's important to take time for "good-byes." Learning how and when to say "good-bye" is a valuable life skill. If care isn't given to the closure process, members may feel abandoned or betrayed instead of content and hopeful.

In general, this "letting go" process begins four sessions before the last group meeting. In addition to guiding the group through some of the suggested closure activities outlined below, the facilitator raises group members' awareness of the approaching end of their time together by starting a countdown during the last three or four sessions: "Looking at the calendar, I notice that we have four (three, two) more sessions."

Closure Mandala
Closing Activity, fourth-to-last session

Objective:

Group members will create a drawing collectively that represents key features of the group experience as they see it in order to begin the process of saying "good-bye."

Materials:

Butcher paper cut into a large circle (at least 36" diameter) and art supplies such as: crayons, felt pens, paints, stickers, rubber stamps, glue, glitter, sequins

Procedure:

Group members are seated in a circle around a work table with the butcher paper and a variety of art supplies in the middle. The facilitator explains that mandala means "circle" in Sanskrit and is a circular drawing in which all designs radiate from a central symbol. Group members are asked to propose a center symbol that best represents the collective journey of the group. This will become the core drawing for a mandala that the group will create together. The group comes to consensus on the centerpiece (examples: star, flower, moon, sun, tear, earth or globe, face, etc.) and someone is chosen by the group to draw it in the middle of the circle of paper.

Next, participants are encouraged to recall experiences they had with the group that have had a particular impact upon them: skills they've learned and now use successfully, problems they have resolved, friendships they have made, feelings they expressed or learned about, etc. The facilitator then asks everyone to create a representation of these key features on the portion of the circle of paper that is in front of them. In a closing discussion, group members share what they have added to the mandala and its significance. The mandala is signed by everyone and hung in the group space as a tribute to the time spent together.

Inquiry:

The facilitator guides the group sharing of information by adapting the questions and statements in the Activity Inquiry Fan to the content of this experience.

Samples:
How does it feel to look at our finished mandala?
Tell about something someone else said that really affected you?
If you were telling a friend about your entire group experience, what would you say?

Magic Wishing Wands
Closing Activity, fourth-to-last session

Objective:

Group participants will construct a magic wand to symbolize wishes they have for themselves, each other, and the world in order to begin to think of taking their newly acquired perspectives from the group into the world at large.

Materials:

15–18" sticks or wooden dowels, cool temperature glue guns and sticks, and art supplies such as: feathers, glitter, sequins, shiny fabric and paper, ribbon

Procedure:

Group members are seated around a work table full of art supplies for free expression. The facilitator explains that each member will be creating a "magic wand" using the materials on the table. Members are asked to think about how they would complete the following statements as they are working on their project:

"One thing I wish for myself is _____."
"A wish that I have for each person in group is _____."
"A wish that I have for _____ is _____."
"A wish that I have for our school (town, community) is _____."
"Something that I wish for the world is _____."

Members share their creations and their wishes. The Magic Wands are taken home to remind them of the group experience.

Inquiry:

The facilitator guides the group sharing of information by adapting the questions and statements in the Activity Inquiry Fan to the content of this experience.

Samples:
Are there any wishes that people made that could come true? How?
Name something in this activity that is about how people feel.
Name something in this activity that is about how people act.
Compare this activity to others that we have done. How are they the same? Different?

Closure Celebration Brainstorm
Closing Activity, third-to-last session

Objective:

Group members will participate in a brainstorming session to plan an end-of-group celebration and ways to keep in touch with each other when the group is over in order to eliminate potential feelings of abandonment related to the end of the group experience.

Materials:

Chart paper and marking pens. Construction paper and crayons or markers.

Procedure:

The facilitator reminds members that the group will be ending in two more weeks and suggests that they might like to plan for a closing party or activity for their next session. Two charts are hung up, one entitled *"What We Want to Do"* and the other labeled *"Who We Want to Invite."* For young children, the most meaningful closure celebrations occur when the facilitator guides group members to invite significant adults in their lives. Adolescents benefit from including a trusted friend, as well. Facilitators need to make sure that someone special attends for each group member.

Members brainstorm ideas, which are recorded on the chart paper. (Possible activities include pizza party, banana-split-making party, potluck lunch, or picnic in the park.) After suggestions have been exhausted, the group comes to consensus on an activity and guest list.

Members make a list of items required for the celebration and volunteer to provide part of what is needed. In addition, each participant creates an invitation(s) for those they wish to invite and agrees to deliver the invitations.

Inquiry:

The facilitator guides the group sharing of information by adapting the questions and statements in the Activity Inquiry Fan to the content of this experience.

Samples:

Name some of the significant peoples others want to invite.
What was the hardest part about planning this event? The easiest? The saddest? The most exciting?
What is the most important thing about the event that we planned, in your opinion?

Closure Celebration
Closing Activity, second-to-last session

See previous activity.

Letting Go Ceremony
Closing Activity, last session

Objective:

Group members will reinforce their sense of connection to the group experience even as they let it go.

Materials:

A basket full of inexpensive "treasures" such as: polished stones, marbles, beach glass, shells, ribbon pieces, large sequins or plastic jewels, little message or inspiration cards. A large clear plastic or glass jar or fish bowl labeled as follows:

Group Memory Jar
The treasures in this jar are gifts from everyone who has ever participated in a group experience such as yours. Now as you add your treasure, you belong to an ever-growing circle of support.

Procedure:

The facilitator asks each group member to select two treasured items from the full basket. Each person around the circle shares the reason for the choices that they made by responding to the following open-ended sentence:

"I chose this treasure because it reminds me of _____, and I chose this one because it makes me think of _____."

Next, group members are asked to decide which treasure they will keep and which they will add to the Group Memory Jar that contains items from all participants of previous groups. Someone in the group reads the inscription on the container:

Group Memory Jar
The treasures in this jar are gifts from everyone who has ever participated in a group experience such as yours. Now as you add your treasure you belong to an ever-growing circle of support.

Then each person adds a treasure to the jar and responds to the following:

" I decided to put this treasure in the Group Memory Jar because _____. I'll keep this one with me."

Inquiry:

The facilitator guides the group sharing of information by adapting the questions and statements in the Activity Inquiry Fan to the content of this experience.

Samples:
How did you feel as we started the Memory Jar activity? At the end of it?
What did it mean to you to add your treasure to the jar full of them from the last groups?
How is our group the same as the other groups? How do you think we are unique from the others?

Open Reflection
Closing Activity, last session

Objective:
Group members will gain a sense of accomplishment and completion by sharing significant events from the group experience.

Materials:
Chart paper and marking pens

Procedure:
The facilitator guides group participants in a discussion about significant learning experiences they've had by making statements and asking questions such as:

"Describe a group activity that was particularly meaningful for you."

"Describe the most powerful moment for you during group."

"What was the hardest thing for you to talk about or hear about in group."

"What did you contribute to the group? What did others in the group give to you?"

Next group members are asked to consider ways that they can keep in touch after group ends. These ideas are recorded. If an address and phone exchange is suggested, the facilitator offers to make copies and distribute the list to each group member.

Finally, the facilitator asks members to describe how they will continue to gain needed support after the group ends. Since some may be included in newly forming groups, some may move into individual counseling, and others will be "on their own," a discussion of why people require different options is valuable to acknowledge any feelings of being left-out or less capable.

Inquiry:
The facilitator guides the group sharing of information by adapting the questions and statements in the Activity Inquiry Fan to the content of this experience.

Samples:
How could you use everything that we learned in group to change something about your life?

What are three ways to get support if you need it after group ends?

How will it feel to keep in touch with people from the group? What if some people choose not to stay in touch?

Now that the group is launched, the facilitator's task is to determine a focus and starting point for the Working Phase of the group process. The facilitator may choose to refer to the self-surveys and behavior checklists from Chapter 2, along with information disclosed during the Opening Phase activities, to determine which People Skill to approach first. Or, the group may move sequentially through the developmental social skills exercises of *Belonging* beginning with *Chapter 5: Exploring Self.*

Facilitator Log

Things to remember:

_____

_____

_____

_____

_____

_____

_____

_____

_____

_____

_____

_____

_____

_____

_____

_____

_____

_____

_____

_____

_____

_____

Section 2:
The Working Stage

Each set of activities in the following chapters are divided into three phases: Awareness, Practice and Transfer. Each phase is progressively more demanding, requiring that group members assume more responsibility for their own development. At the Awareness phase, concepts and information are introduced through a closely guided group activity. At the Practice phase, the work done at the previous level is reinforced and mastery of specific People Skills is emphasized. Transfer phase experiences are designed to encourage group members to apply their new knowledge and skills outside of the group.

Some of the activities are applicable to all ages. Some are presented in a Level I and Level II format. The Level I version is for younger and/or less mature groups and Level II is for an older and/or more sophisticated group composition.

The Activity Inquiry Fan presented in Chapter 1 is meant to be used by the group facilitator or co-facilitator as a means of promoting self-disclosure and discussion during and after all of the activities in the Belonging Program. The questions and statements require progressively more advanced thinking from the simplest (Knowledge, Comprehension, and Application) through the more complex (Analysis, Synthesis, and Evaluation). The more group members interact with the concepts and People Skills presented in a given session, the more likely they are to integrate these new ideas and tools into their everyday lives.

Exploring
Self

Chapter 5

Self-exploration, an introspective journey to discover more about who we are as individuals, provides the basis for meaningful interactions with others. One desired outcome of the experiences included in this section is a greater degree of self-awareness. From this improved self-knowledge springs increased self-acceptance. Both lead to a secure belief in unlimited potential for growth and a new appreciation and celebration of self. Over time, members are guided to see that higher degrees of self-awareness, self-acceptance, and appreciation of self provide a solid foundation for positive, meaningful interactions and connections with others. It also becomes apparent that without such a personal foundation, healthy relationships with others and success in group settings is not likely to occur.

Set I. Purpose:
To increase self-awareness, acceptance, and appreciation

Self-Surveys
Awareness

Objective
Groups members will complete a list of questions and open-ended statements designed to promote self-awareness.

Materials
Self Surveys (Experiences 5.1 and 5.2), pencils

Procedure
Group members complete the survey sheets—Level I for younger/less mature groups, and Level II for older/more sophisticated groups. As always, sharing is voluntary.

Inquiry
The facilitator guides the group sharing of information by adapting the questions and statements in the Activity Inquiry Fan to the content of this experience.

Samples:
Tell us something that you learned about yourself?
What do you think is the main point of this activity?
How did you feel at the beginning of the survey? Now how do you feel?

Name _____

Grade _____ Age _____ Date _____

Self-Survey
Level I

Mark the answer that best describes you:	Yes	Sometimes	No
1. I know what I can do well. [ES]	( )	( )	( )
2. I enjoy talking with people. [SI]	( )	( )	( )
3. I tell people how I feel. [FF]	( )	( )	( )
4. I get along with other kids. [MF]	( )	( )	( )
5. I like to play games with others. [CO]	( )	( )	( )
6. I have trouble asking for things. [AY]	( )	( )	( )
7. I share my ideas even if someone laughs at me. [HV]	( )	( )	( )
8. I get upset when things don't go my way. [MS]	( )	( )	( )
9. I know what to do when I have a problem. [RC]	( )	( )	( )

Key:
AY–Asserting Yourself
CO–Cooperating with Others
ES–Exploring Self
FF–Focusing on Feelings
HV–Handling Verbal Abuse

MF–Making Friends
MS–Managing Strong Feelings
RC–Resolving Conflicts
SI–Sharing Ideas

Name _____

Grade _____ **Age** _____ **Date** _____

Self-Survey, Level II

Mark the answer that best describes you:

	Always	Sometimes	Never
1. I get along well with others. [ES]	( )	( )	( )
2. It's hard for me to talk to people. [SI]	( )	( )	( )
3. It's easy for me to share my feelings with others. [FF]	( )	( )	( )
4. I have friends whom I trust. [MF]	( )	( )	( )
5. I like to get together with friends. [CO]	( )	( )	( )
6. It is difficult for me to tell people what I need or want. [AY]	( )	( )	( )
7. I share my ideas even when someone laughs. [HV]	( )	( )	( )
8. I spend a lot of time thinking about mistakes I've made. [MS]	( )	( )	( )
9. I ask people to help me solve problems. [RC]	( )	( )	( )

Complete the following sentences:

1. The thing I do best is _____.[ES]

2. When I meet someone new, I _____.[SI]

3. Today I am feeling _____.[FF]

4. I know someone is my friend when _____.[MF]

5. When someone in charge gives me a direction, I feel _____.[CO]

6. When I need help, I _____.[AY]

7. When someone is rude to me, I _____.[HV]

8. When things don't go my way, I _____.[MS]

9. When I have a problem, I _____.[RC]

Key:

AY–Asserting Yourself
CO–Cooperating with Others
ES–Exploring Self
FF–Focusing on Feelings
HV–Handling Verbal Abuse

MF–Making Friends
MS–Managing Strong Feelings
RC–Resolving Conflicts
SI–Sharing Ideas

Hot Seat
Practice

Objective
All group members will receive and then give positive messages about themselves to encourage self-acceptance and appreciation.

Materials
Tall stool or chair, slips of paper, timer, felt pens or pencils

Procedure
Part I:

Group members write their names on slips of paper and give these to the facilitator. From the collected papers the facilitator chooses one name. The chosen person sits on the stool, or "hot seat," and listens as group members "bombard" the individual with positive comments. Statements made are in sentence form or, to speed the input, just one-word items such as "kind," "smart," "polite," etc. Having a list of suggested descriptive words on display helps start the process. One group member keeps time as the spotlighted person takes in the information for one minute. The "hot seat" person is then directed to say "Thank you" and nothing more. The leader guides the process by encouraging eye contact, relaxed body posture, no verbal reactions, and a continual flow of positive information. The activity is carried out until each group member has had a turn.

Part II:

Next, the facilitator again randomly chooses a person by drawing a name. This person sits on the "hot seat" and begins to relate personal strengths to the group. A group member times the process for one minute. The facilitator provides a format to follow, such as "I am a person who _____" or "I can _____." The facilitator redirects someone who says, "I think I can" to say, "I can _____." During each person's minute the facilitator might interject new formats, such as "Now, just say single words that describe you." As with any activity, anyone may pass.

Inquiry
The facilitator guides the group sharing of information by adapting the questions and statements in the Activity Inquiry Fan to the content of this experience.

Samples:
Tell three things people said about you.
What was the hardest/easiest part of this activity for you?
Explain why you think this activity has the title "Hot Seat."

Pride in Self
Transfer

Objective

Group members will write positive statements about themselves to reveal an increased level of self-awareness, acceptance, and appreciation.

Materials

"Pride Sheet" (Experience 5.3)

Procedure

At the end of the group meeting, the facilitator gives each member a "Pride Sheet" and asks members to fill it out and share it with someone that they trust (e.g., a parent, teacher, or best friend), or keep it for personal reflection.

Inquiry

The facilitator guides the group sharing of information by adapting the questions and statements in the Activity Inquiry Fan to the content of this experience.

Samples:

What do you think is the main point of this activity?
What is one thing you learned about other group members?
Would you recommend this activity to people in another group? Why or why not?

Pride Sheet

This Pride Sheet belongs to _____.

I am proud of myself because I am_____

_____.

The one thing that I am especially proud of is _____

_____.

I felt good when I _____

_____.

I am pleased to have _____ for a friend.

I am unique because I can _____

_____.

I deserve recognition for _____

_____.

Set II. Purpose:
To look at one's life to date and recognize primary connections

Family Tree
Awareness

Objective
Group members will complete a Family Tree chart indicating those people they consider to be part of their family.

Materials
Family Tree charts (Experience 5.4), pencils or felt pens and chart paper, or chalkboard and chalk

Procedure
The group begins with a discussion of how each person defines "family." For each member, the facilitator records the definition, which will be referred to when the activity is completed. All participants are given a Family Tree chart (Experience 5.4) and directed to write their own names on the trunk and fill in the names of those perceived as being part of their family, according to personal definitions, since many do not live in a traditional family structure. All members are encouraged to view their family systems as unique and not strange or unacceptable. When everyone is finished, group members read their definitions of "family" and share what they wrote or drew on their chart.

Variation: Group members draw their own image of a tree and fill in the names of their family members, as described above.

Inquiry
The facilitator guides the group sharing of information by adapting the questions and statements in the Activity Inquiry Fan to the content of this experience.

Samples:
Who are the most important people on your Family Tree?
Pretend that we know nothing about you. Describe your family to us.
How is our group like a family?

Family Tree

Lifeline Practice
Practice

Objective

Group members will relate a one-minute autobiography to promote a sense of connection with significant life events.

Materials

"Lifeline" (Experience 5.5), pencils, timer

Procedure

Group members consider highlights of their lives to date. Each writes notes or draws pictures about these on the "Lifeline" sheet (Experience 5.5). When this is complete, everyone is given two minutes each to relate important elements of their lives to the rest of the group. Additional time is given for questions group members may have for the person who's sharing.

Variation: Group members draw a visual representation of their life as if it were a trail map. They are encouraged to include markers for significant life events along the path, beginning with their birth.

Inquiry

The facilitator guides the group sharing of information by adapting the questions and statements in the Activity Inquiry Fan to the content of this experience.

Samples:

Make up a title for your life experiences to date.

Name one thing from your Lifeline or Trail Map that is about how people feel and one thing about how they act.

What is the single most important experience of your life?

Lifeline

Cooperative Story
More Practice

Objective

Group members will gain a sense of connection with others in the group by sharing significant life events from birth to present age in a cooperative story.

Materials

None

Procedure

The facilitator begins the exercise by taking one minute to tell a significant personal experience about birth and instructs the next person to tell something which happened at several months of age. The next person picks up the story by adding an event from the first year of life. The story appears to be about one person who is really a composite of everyone present.

A sample story might read:

Facilitator: I was born prematurely in an emergency room in a hospital in Boise, Idaho.

Person 2: When I was three months old, I was in Mexico City with my family. We lived there until I was two years old. I spoke both English and Spanish.

Person 3: When I was two years old, my twin sisters were born. I remember feeling very left out, but my grandfather paid special attention to me.

Person 4: I cut off all of my hair when I was three. My mother cried and cried and taped ribbons on my head …

The story continues until the "composite person" reaches the age of the youngest group member.

Last Person: On my eighteenth birthday, I went on a solo hike in the Sierras. I kept a journal of my experiences.

Inquiry

The facilitator guides the group sharing of information by adapting the questions and statements in the Activity Inquiry Fan to the content of this experience.

Samples:
Recall a significant event from the beginning of "our" life, from the middle, from the present.
Give "our" life story a title.
What do you wish would happen next in "our" life story?

Name Search
Transfer

Objective

Group members will gain a sense of personal uniqueness and connection to their family story by researching the significance of their names.

Materials

None

Procedure

Group members are asked to explore the origins of their first, middle, and/or last names in conversation with other members of their family. Were they named after someone? Who? What is his/her story? What nationalities are represented by their names? What does their first name mean? Do they ever think about changing their name(s)? If so, to what?

Set III. Purpose:

To acknowledge personal growth during the group experience

Note: Journals are used in transfer activities throughout the People Skills training after their function is established here. Young children especially relate to the idea of having an "empty book" to be "filled up" with their thoughts and feelings in words and pictures.

Journals in History
Awareness

Objective

Group members will discuss the concept of empty books/journals and brainstorm possible uses for them as related to their group experience.

Materials

Journals (cloth-bound, spiral-bound) or materials for making a handmade journal: construction paper, blank writing paper, stapler, marking pens

Procedure

The facilitator directs a discussion about the history of diaries and journals after each member is given or makes one. The focus is on how they have been used historically or traditionally. Next, group members are asked to consider the history of the group experience so far and to write or draw about this as the first entry in their journal. They are guided to date each entry so that they are able to track their "travels" with the group over time.

Inquiry

The facilitator guides the group sharing of information by adapting the questions and statements in the Activity Inquiry Fan to the content of this experience.

Samples:

How were diaries and journals used in the past? (Documentation of travels, discoveries, wars, personal feelings)
How is our group experience like a journey or a discovery?
What possibilities are there for using journals in our group? What kinds of things could we include?

Journal Writing Exercises
Practice

Objective

Group members will complete a self-exploration activity to begin using journals as a means of tracking personal and collective growth.

Materials

Journals, pens, pencils, felt pens

Procedure

The following is a list of topics to stimulate the use of journals as tools for self-discovery. Group members are given the following list of topics and are asked to choose one or more to complete during the group session. The rest of the suggestions can be taken home and worked with as an individual chooses.

1. Tell or draw about your likes and dislikes.
2. Draw or tell about someplace you'd really like to go. Tell or show who would go with you.
3. Think back in time. Draw or write a vivid memory you have of either a pleasant or unpleasant event.
4. Draw or write an ending for these unfinished sentences:

Level I	*Level II*
At school I _____	After high school, I _____
Friends are _____	Friends are _____
I know how to _____	A good relationship is _____
I like it when _____	I am happiest when _____
Sharing is _____	I really know how to _____
My family _____	Family is_____
I am smart when I _____	Being smart is _____

5. Make a list or draw about things you would change if you could.
6. Describe or draw a favorite daydream.
7. List five things you would never change about yourself.
8. If I could be anything I wanted to be, I would _____.
9. One thing about myself I'd really like to change is _____. I'll start changing by _____.
10. I wish that I _____.
11. Write a thank-you note to someone in your past.
12. Describe a relationship that ended or changed. How did you feel?
13. Describe or draw someone who is very special to you. Tell why that person is so special.
14. One way I deal with loneliness is _____.
15. Plan at least one special treat for yourself each day of the week. Write these down. Example:

    Sunday—Play softball with John.

    Monday—Go for a walk by myself.

    Tuesday—Buy myself a frozen yogurt.

Inquiry

The facilitator guides the group sharing of information by adapting the questions and statements in the Activity Inquiry Fan to the content of this experience.

Samples:
What do you think is the main point of this activity?
What part of the activity was the most significant and/or most challenging for you?
Think of another journal entry topic.

Journal Writing: Metaphor
Transfer

Objective

To deepen their understanding of personal uniqueness, group members will write about themselves as an object in nature.

Materials

Journals, pencils, pens

Procedure

As an outside assignment, group members are asked to select an object in nature, such as a tree, rock, stone, or blade of grass and to write about themselves as if they were that object. Members may also choose to draw what they would look like being the object. Members write in their journals describing in detail what they see around them and how it feels to be that object. They expand this daily by writing down or drawing about something they imagine experiencing as this object.

Set IV. Purpose:

To encourage group members to affirm their personal strengths and to identify areas for improvement

What You Say
Awareness

Objective

Group members will use self-affirming language as one means of achieving desired behavior change.

Materials

Support Cards (Experience 5.6), pencils

Procedure

The facilitator explains to members that supportive language consists of positive statements people make about themselves or others. The group discusses real-life examples of how nonsupportive thoughts and words lessen one's ability to take action and bring about desired results. Supportive, self-affirming thoughts and language help people accomplish personal goals or change.

Group members make lists of five to ten realistic goal statements. Some examples include:

1. I will get more things accomplished.
2. I will be friendly to those I meet.
3. I will learn how to study for tests.

Next, members use their goals as a starting place for creating supportive statements. These sentences consist of positive, first-person, present tense, action words, such as:

1. I am an action person. I finish what I start and I know I do it well.
2. I am able to be warm and friendly when I meet others, and I know others respect me for it.
3. I am a person who studies well for tests, and I am rewarded with good grades.

Group members read the "Support Cards" to themselves and to the group. Blank "Support Cards" are made available at each group meeting for use by anyone who comes to the session feeling "down" or disheartened.

Inquiry

The facilitator guides the group sharing of information by adapting the questions and statements in the Activity Inquiry Fan to the content of this experience.

Samples:

Explain why you think this activity is called "What You Say?"

Would you recommend this activity to people in another group? Why?

Make up a new activity that you could use to teach your friends what we learned about using "Support Cards."

Support Cards

"I am_____

_____

_____."

"I am able to _____

_____

_____."

"I am a person who _____

_____

_____."

Inside Out
Practice

Objective

Group members will depict personal qualities and areas of desired change to help them grow and improve in desired ways.

Materials

Manila file folders, Support Cards (Experience 5.6), magazine pictures, glue, pencils, felt pens, glitter, sequins, stickers, etc.

Procedure

The facilitator explains that everyone has a private and a public side. In this activity the inside of the file folder represents the "inside," or private, part of themselves; and the outside of the file folder stands for the "outside," or public, aspect.

Inside: Group members are asked to create a collage of drawings, magazine pictures, symbols, etc. that represents both their inner qualities (what they know about themselves that no one else might know) and areas of desired change (those things that they wish were different).

Outside: Next, members continue the collage on the outside of the folder by depicting both their public qualities (what they show others and/or what they know others think about them) and areas of desired change (those things in their daily public lives that they wish could be improved or altered).

Members share the content of their collages with the rest of the group. The group helps each person identify several areas of desired change that could realistically happen. Participants use the "Support Cards" (Experience 5.6) to develop supportive statements as a first step toward achieving desired improvements and/or change.

Inquiry

The facilitator guides the group sharing of information by adapting the questions and statements in the Activity Inquiry Fan to the content of this experience.

Samples:

What are three things that you learned about other group members by sharing this activity?
What part of this activity was hardest/easiest?
What do you think is the main point of this activity?

Support One Another
Transfer

Objective

Group members will independently show support for others in group.

Materials

3x5 index cards

Procedure

The facilitator instructs group members to write a supportive statement to give to another group member some time before the next group session. Some sentence stems that could be used are:

"I know that you _____."

"I admire you for working hard to _____."

"I'm sure that you _____."

The supportive comments can be written on the index card and handed to the person or said directly.

The process of self-exploration is lifelong. By returning to self-study exercises and reviewing journals throughout the People Skills program, group members become aware of how they view themselves and life circumstances differently over time and with new experiences. They begin to see that everyone's life is a journey, rarely static, and usually changing. In order to continually learn and grow throughout a lifetime, the ability to communicate both as a clear speaker and careful listener is essential. Basic communication themes are addressed in *Chapter 6: Sharing Ideas.*

Facilitator Log

Things to remember:

_____

_____

_____

_____

_____

_____

_____

_____

_____

_____

_____

_____

_____

_____

_____

_____

_____

_____

_____

_____

Sharing
Ideas

Chapter 6

Meaningful exchanges are more likely to occur when Communication Basics—the details of both careful listening and clear speaking—are practiced and mastered. From this simple but essential foundation, facility with In-depth Communication Tools enhances the quality of the verbal and non-verbal interactions participants have within the group and in their daily lives. Communication Basics and the In-depth Communication Tools of paraphrasing, reflective listening, constructive responses, and self-disclosure are explored in the following series of group experiences.

Set I. Purpose:

To establish a foundation of Communication Basics from which more in-depth skills can be learned

Maze Mania
Awareness

Objective

Group members will identify speaking and listening skills required to send and receive clear communications.

Materials

"Maze Mania" (Experience 6.1), pencil, chart paper, felt marker

Procedure

The facilitator asks group members to partner with someone and sit across from each other at a table. One person carefully directs the other through the maze (Experience 6.1) by giving clear oral directions. Clarifying questions are encouraged. After all participants have successfully completed the maze, the facilitator leads a discussion to draw from the group the specific behaviors the listener and speaker did to complete the task. This information is recorded and referred to when beginning the next Practice Activity— Communication Basics.

Inquiry

The facilitator guides the group sharing of information by adapting the questions and statements in the Activity Inquiry Fan to the content of this experience.

Samples:

What was the most important thing your partner said or did to accomplish the completion of the maze?
Name three directions your partner gave? Were they helpful? Why or why not?
Name a question that your partner asked that helped clarify a direction.
Did you feel as if you and your partner were a team? Why or why not?
How did you know that your partner was listening to you?

Maze Mania

ENTER

EXIT

EXIT

Communication Basics
Practice

Objective

Group members will identify and practice Listening and Speaking Communication Basics to form a strong foundation for the mastery of In-depth Communication Tools.

Materials

Communication Basics Checklist (Experience 6.2)

Procedure

The facilitator leads a discussion of the listening and speaking components of Communication Basics as recorded from the previous activity and as presented in Experience 6.2. The facilitator explains and demonstrates each behavior. Modeling is an essential technique for learning effective listening and speaking skills.

Group members form triads, with each person choosing the role of either listener, speaker, or observer. The facilitator gives the observers copies of the Communication Basics checklist and asks the speaker to select a topic from the list below. Speakers talk about their chosen topic for one minute. During this time, the listener and the speaker practice the newly introduced skills outlined on the Communication Basics checklist. The observer watches the listener and the speaker and checks off skills that are being used. At the end of the timed session, the observer shares the checklist notations made with the other two. Positions are rotated until each member has had an opportunity to try each role.

Suggested Topics:
1. A memorable trip
2. A special friend
3. A hope for the future
4. An embarrassing moment
5. A frightening experience
6. Someone you admire

Inquiry

The facilitator guides the group sharing of information by adapting the questions and statements in the Activity Inquiry Fan to the content of this experience.

Samples:
What do you think is the main point of this activity?
Tell about something that the speaker shared?
How does this activity relate to you and your friends?

Communication Basics Checklist

Listening

1. Establish Eye Contact
- Look directly at the speaker without staring.

2. Acknowledge the Speaker

Verbal:
- "Uh-huh." "M-m-m."
- "That sounds good."
- "I see …"

Nonverbal:
- Nod.
- Smile.

3. Use Supportive "Listening" Body Language
- Sit upright/straight.
- Turn your body toward the speaker.
- Lean forward slightly.
- Maintain an open posture (arms uncrossed, relaxed).

4. Pay Careful Attention
- Keep respectfully silent when someone speaks.
- Give the speaker your complete attention.
- Ask clarifying questions only when necessary.
- Avoid interrupting.

5. Establish a "Social Space" with the Speaker
- Keep within an arm's length in one-to-one and small group settings.
- Adjust the distance to fit the circumstance

Speaking

1. Maintain Eye Contact with Listener/Audience
- Look in the direction of the listener/audience most of the time.

2. Speak Clearly
- Think about what you want to say before speaking.
- Enunciate.
- Be specific and stay on track.
- Check for understanding.

3. Exercise Appropriate Volume
- Speak loudly enough to be heard.
- Adjust the volume to fit the situation.

4. Use Expressive "Speaking" Body Language
- Turn your body toward the listener/audience.
- Use hand gestures and facial expression to enhance the verbal message.

5. Establish a "Social Space" with the Listener
- Adjust the distance to fit the circumstance, closer for one-to-one or small groups and further away for larger groups.

Copycat
More Practice

Objective

Group members will gain more experience with Communication Basics by giving and receiving directions needed to complete a drawing.

Materials

Drawing paper, felt pens

Procedure

Group members are instructed to draw a simple design on a blank piece of paper and not show it to anyone. Next the facilitator gives each person another blank sheet of paper. One group member stands before the group and gives clear verbal instructions to the others to have them draw replicas of the speaker's design. Group members receiving directions are permitted to ask clarifying questions. The speaker may show and tell only in response to questions from the group. Otherwise the instructions are given using words alone, without any gestures or demonstrations. The activity continues until each group member has had an opportunity to give instructions to the rest of the group.

Inquiry

The facilitator guides the group sharing of information by adapting the questions and statements in the Activity Inquiry Fan to the content of this experience.

Samples:

Explain the hardest and the easiest part of this activity.
What would have helped you get your directions across better?
Which Communication Basics were used to perform this activity?

Journal Entry: Communication Basics
Transfer

Objective

Group members will practice Communication Basics away from the group and record their experiences and feelings.

Materials

Journals, pens

Procedure

The facilitator asks group members to write or draw in their journals during the next week to describe (1) a time when they really listened to someone else, (2) a time when they didn't feel listened to by others, or (3) a time when they explained something very well to another person.

Set II. Purpose:

To develop the ability to paraphrase and reflect feelings to gain skill with In-depth Communication Tools related to listening

Paraphrasing and Reflecting
Awareness

Objective

Group members will learn information about the in-depth listening tools of paraphrasing and reflecting feelings to increase their overall communication abilities.

Materials

A collection of library books with lots of dialogue among characters

Procedure

The facilitator explains that there are two simple but significant ways to let someone know that you are listening to them: paraphrasing and reflecting feelings.
- *Paraphrasing* occurs when a listener restates the key features of what someone said. It is used to clarify information, solidify agreements, and check that a message was received as intended. "What I think you said is _____. Correct?"
- *Reflecting feelings* happens when the listener brings forward the expressed or implied emotion in someone's message. "When you talked about _____, it sounded as if you were feeling _____."

Next, members of the group choose books from the library collection. A volunteer reads a passage and the facilitator paraphrases the content and reflects the feeling expressed or implied in the selection. Participants form pairs and take turns with one person reading a passage and the other paraphrasing and reflecting the feelings of the characters in the book.

Inquiry

The facilitator guides the group sharing of information by adapting the questions and statements in the Activity Inquiry Fan to the content of this experience.

Samples:
What is the easiest/hardest part of paraphrasing what someone says?
What helped you guess how a character was feeling?
When and where do you think that you could use paraphrasing and reflecting feelings?

My Garden of Influence
Practice

Objective   Note: This activity is to be carried out over two group sessions.

Session 1: Group members will become proficient at paraphrasing information shared by another person to develop in-depth listening skills.

Session 2: Group members will become proficient at paraphrasing information and reflecting the feelings shared by another person to develop in-depth listening skills.

Materials

Drawing paper, felt pens, crayons, pencils

Procedure

Session 1: Group members are asked to draw a picture of themselves as if they were a plant. Also included in the drawing are other objects in nature that share their environment.

Next, pairs are formed and one member of the duo listens as the other shows and tells about his/her drawing and then addresses the following inquiry:

• In your life, who are the significant people who share your environment, and how have they influenced you?

When the speaker has finished, the listener paraphrases or restates in his or her own words the key features of what the speaker shared. The facilitator suggests the following sentence starters for the listener to use while paraphrasing what was heard:

"What I heard you say is _____. Is that right?"

"What I think you said is _____. Did I understand you correctly?"

Partners switch roles so that each person is able to be both speaker and listener. The facilitator collects the drawings to be used again during the second session of this activity.

Inquiry

The facilitator guides the group sharing of information by adapting the questions and statements in the Activity Inquiry Fan to the content of this experience.

Samples:

Some people think that listening is the most important part of communication and that it is a "lost art." What do you think they mean?

How did it feel to have someone listen so attentively to you that s/he could paraphrase the important features of your sharing?

What are some situations in your life that would benefit by you becoming a skilled listener?

Procedure

Session 2: Group members are given back their drawings and are asked to add the forces of nature that influence their plant (e.g., the sun, rain, wind, clouds, fire, lightning, etc.).

When everyone has finished, pairs are formed again. The speaker now tells about his/her drawing and includes information in response to the following inquiries:

1) What or whom represents the sun in your life—someone or something that really "shines" in your mind?
2) What or whom is the rain in your life—someone or something who "waters" you, and gives you life support when you need it?
3) What or whom is the soil in your life—someone or something who "feeds" you when you really need to be nurtured and cared for?
4) What or whom is any of the other forces of nature in your life? Tell about that.

When the speaker is done sharing, the listener once again paraphrases what was said, this time also reflecting the feelings (either stated or implied) in the message. The facilitator suggests the following formats for reflecting feelings.

"When you shared about _____, it sounded as if you felt _____."
"When you said that _____, I sensed that you were feeling _____."
"From what you said about _____, I wonder if you might be feeling _____."

Partners switch roles so that each has a turn to be both speaker and listener.

Inquiry

The facilitator guides the group sharing of information by adapting the questions and statements in the Activity Inquiry Fan to the content of this experience.

Samples:

Some people think many big problems could be solved if we listened to each other more. What does this mean to you?

Name one relationship that you have that could be improved if you practiced paraphrasing and reflecting feelings?

What was the best part of this activity? What do you think your partner would say was the best part? Why?

A Listening Ear
Transfer

Objective
Group members will record in their journals examples of the most important words that they listen to during the next week to assist in keeping the value of skilled listening in mind.

Materials
Journal, pen or pencil, colored markers

Procedure
Group members are instructed to draw a picture of an ear or a face with big ears—either a human or another animal's—in their journals. During the upcoming week, they are asked to write or draw about significant information that they listened to in their daily activities, as if the sentences were entering the ears in their journal drawing.

Set III. Purpose:

To develop the ability to deliver a constructive response and a self-disclosure in order to gain skill with In-depth Communication Tools related to speaking

Fact or Opinion? Ideas or Advice?
Awareness

Objective

Group members will label statements as being fact or opinion, ideas or advice to learn aspects of a constructive response—one that is honest without being judgmental and/or threatening.

Materials

"Fact/Opinion, Ideas/Advice" sheets (Experiences 6.3 and 6.4)

Procedure

The facilitator leads a discussion concerning the difference between fact and opinion: (1) "fact" is defined as something generally agreed to be true, and (2) "opinion" is a viewpoint held to be true by one person or a particular group. The discussion moves next to considering ideas and advice: (1) "an idea," whether fact or opinion, is presented for consideration without requiring agreement or any action on the part of the receiver, and (2) "advice," on the other hand, is wrought with "shoulds" and "oughts," whether stated or implied. The facilitator points out that personal judgments, biases, and expectations are imposed upon others when opinions are presented as indisputable facts and creative ideas are lost in advice-giving.

After discussing the above-mentioned distinctions, group members individually complete the appropriate level of "Fact or Opinion, Idea or Advice?" sheet (Experiences 6.3 and 6.4). A discussion to compare conclusions and to discover "gray areas" serves as a follow-up.

Inquiry

The facilitator guides the group sharing of information by adapting the questions and statements in the Activity Inquiry Fan to the content of this experience.

Samples:

Compare facts and opinions or ideas and advice. How are they the same and how are they different?

Tell about any disagreements that occurred during this activity.

How does it feel to have someone give you advice as opposed to offer you an opinion or share an idea?

Fact or Opinion? Ideas or Advice?
Level I

Mark sentences "F" for fact or "O" for opinion.

_____ Friendships last forever.

_____ Teachers care about students.

_____ Reading is fun.

_____ Many children have parents who work outside of the home.

_____ Many schools have after-school programs for students.

_____ Kids love animals.

_____ Some animals are in danger of becoming extinct.

_____ Flowering plants are alive.

_____ People love to swim.

Mark sentences "I" for ideas or "A" for advice.

_____ You ought to get a spelling tutor.

_____ There are some good computer programs to help correct spelling errors.

_____ You should join a sports team instead of staying indoors so much.

_____ I hear Sandy is a good volleyball coach. It might be fun to join the team.

_____ You shouldn't eat so many sweets.

_____ A balanced diet promotes good health.

_____ You ought to get a haircut. That purple color is weird.

_____ I found haircuts I like in this magazine.

_____ I've heard there are great exhibits at the fair this year.

_____ You need to get over your fear of crowds and come to the fair.

Fact or Opinion? Ideas or Advice?
Level II

Mark sentences "F" for fact or "O" for opinion.

_____ You are your own best friend.

_____ Smoking is hazardous to your health.

_____ Depression is a feeling of deep sorrow.

_____ Everyone loves to dance.

_____ Friends can be trusted.

_____ Cocaine is addictive.

_____ 50-70% of all marriages end in divorce.

_____ Life is fun.

_____ Swimming is an excellent form of exercise.

Mark sentences "I" for idea or "A" for advice.

_____ Everyone needs to follow "The Golden Rule."

_____ You might consider seeing a dietician or nutritionist about your stomach trouble.

_____ You should get to a doctor now.

_____ There is growing evidence linking depression and alcoholism.

_____ Many parents want the best for their children.

_____ You ought to care for your pets better by giving them daily vitamins.

_____ You would get better grades if you turned the TV off when you did homework.

_____ Exercise would help you keep that weight off. You should join a health club.

_____ Everyone ought to have a job. No wonder you feel bored.

_____ I hear there are quite a few summer jobs available in the community.

Constructive Responses
Practice

Objective
Group members will practice making constructive responses in the form of opinions and ideas.

Materials
Role-Play sheets (Experiences 6.5 and 6.6)

Procedure
Group members listen to a role play between two volunteers. One presents a dilemma from Experiences 6.5 or 6.6 and the other offers a constructive response. The respondent is given time to construct a thoughtful response using the formats noted on the Role-Play Sheet: "In my opinion, _____," "One idea I have is _____," or "Have you considered _____?" The facilitator reminds group members that information given using this type of language does not threaten or judge the listener, and thus encourages open communication. "This-is-how-it-is" type responses aren't usually well received and, therefore, do little to promote the process of communication.

Inquiry
The facilitator guides the group sharing of information by adapting the questions and statements in the Activity Inquiry Fan to the content of this experience.

Samples:
Which response had the most merit for you?
Share two ways learning to respond in this manner will help you in your daily life.
Explain why responses such as these are called "constructive." What might a "destructive" response sound like?

Role-Play Situations: Sharing Ideas
Level I

1. My teacher always chooses me to answer questions in class. I like being called on, but the other kids mock me because of it.

One idea I have is _____ .

2. I really want to play the guitar, but my parents can't afford the instrument. They said maybe in a few years I will be able to have lessons, but I'm ready now.

In my opinion _____ .

3. I have a hard time eating the hot lunches at school, but my dad thinks it's the best way for me to get a balanced meal. He works late and says it's easier for him to give me lunch money than to make lunches every day.

Have you considered _____ ?

4. I'm really struggling in my reading group. Every time I get called on to read out loud I clam up. Part of our grade is for oral reading.

Have you tried _____ .

Role-Play Situations: Sharing Ideas
Level II

1. One of my friends dislikes my other friends. She says that I have to decide between my other friends and her. I don't want to make a decision like that.

In my opinion _____.

2. My friend John laughs about my new boyfriend, who is very shy. I wish he liked my new boyfriend.

Have you considered _____?

3. My mother has promised me a new wardrobe if I lose 20 pounds. I like how I look just the way that I am. Still, I want to please my mother.

One idea I have is _____.

4. I stayed out past my curfew once last year. Now, almost a year later, my dad still brings it up every time I go out. I'd really like him to trust me more.

Have you tried _____?

"Put-Downs"
More Practice

Objective

Group members will create constructive responses which contain a critical component in order to learn to convey a sensitive message without it being perceived as a put-down.

Materials

Slips of paper, pencils, pens

Procedure

The facilitator reviews the features of constructive responses gleaned from the previous two experiences and adds that such responses may also include an element of helpful criticism. Such constructive criticism of someone's actions is accomplished (1) with the listeners permission, (2) with the intention of being helpful and encouraging, and (3) by pointing out the possible benefits of the suggested behavior change.

Next, the facilitator points out that sometimes critical comments are made without permission, good intention, or regard for a beneficial outcome. Such put-downs are not constructive responses because they usually attack the person involved rather than focus on behavior that can be changed.

Group members are asked to write examples of put-downs on the slips of paper provided, one per paper. The facilitator gives samples such as:

1. "How stupid can you get?"
2. "I cannot believe you did that!"
3. "Couldn't you think of anything else but that?"
4. "He thinks you're a jerk."

The put-downs are collected. Each group member draws one and takes a turn reading it to the group and asking how it would feel to have the comments actually directed toward them. Members then are asked to think of a time when they have heard one or more of these "put-downs" used. They then write or verbally express an alternate way of suggesting a beneficial behavior change to someone in that situation.

They are guided to remember to:

(1) ask permission,
(2) focus on behavior that could be changed and the benefits of the change, and
(3) make sure their intention is to be helpful.

For example:

Put-down: "Grow up, Carol! Stop being such a cry baby!"

Constructive Criticism: "Could I make a suggestion, Carol? (permission) How is crying helping this situation? Maybe you could ignore Janet and spend time with the people who care about you. (behavior change) She might stop teasing you if she thought it didn't bother you." (possible benefit)

Inquiry

The facilitator guides the group sharing of information by adapting the questions and statements in the Activity Inquiry Fan to the content of this experience.

Samples:

Think of a time when someone offered you some constructive criticism? How did you receive it?

What is the hardest thing about offering constructive criticism to a friend? What is the hardest thing about listening to constructive criticism addressed to you?

Name three people whose ideas and opinions you are most willing to hear? Why?

Dear Katy!
Transfer

Objective

Group members will write a constructive response to a request for help to further their working knowledge of the language required to do that successfully.

Materials

Journals, copy of "Dear Katy!" letter (Experiences 6.7 and 6.8)

Procedure

Before the next meeting, group members are asked to write a constructive response in their journals as if they were advice columnists answering the pleas of the people in the "Dear Katy!" letters (Experience 6.7 and 6.8).

Dear Katy!
Level I

Dear Katy,

My sister and I earn a weekly allowance for doing certain chores. I do mine; she doesn't do hers. We both still get the money. She promises to do better next week. Week after week she says this. I feel cheated. If I complain, she gets really angry with me. Help!

Fed Up in Los Angeles

Dear Fed Up,

One idea I have is _____

_____

_____

_____

_____

Dear Katy!
Level II

Dear Katy,

I think people should "pay their own way." When my friends and I go out together, I expect each of us to pay our own expenses. One of my friends makes about half as much money as I do, so he doesn't always join in the social activities. I could easily afford to pay his way but don't want to get in the habit of doing that. He also might be offended if I offer. I don't have as much fun without him, though. What can I do?

50/50 in San Luis Obispo

Dear 50/50,

Have you considered _____

_____

_____

_____

_____?

Set IV. Purpose:

To develop the ability to make clear self-disclosures in order to gain skill at In-depth Communication Tools related to speaking

Picture Window
Awareness

Objective

Group members share information about themselves in picture form to learn how self-disclosures promote their personal and social development, as well as that of the group as a whole.

Materials

11x17 drawing paper folded into quarters, colored pens

Procedure

Members are asked to see the paper as a large window with four panes, each representing levels of self-awareness. Group members draw pictures in each quadrant of the paper according to the following set of directions:

1. In the top left pane, draw a picture of something you know about yourself and everyone in the group knows as well.
2. In the bottom left pane, draw a picture of something you know about yourself and others don't know (a secret you have that you wouldn't mind sharing).
3. Close your eyes, what do you see? Draw a picture of it in the top right pane.
4. In the bottom right pane, draw a picture of something unknown, such as a design, abstract sketch, or imagined patterns. In other words, draw a picture of something no one would recognize or know.

Group members share their drawings and discuss how we all have: (1) aspects of ourselves that are common knowledge, (2) secrets or things that no one else knows about us, (3) "blind spots" or things we don't see in ourselves, and (4) possibilities that are completely unknown to us because of lack of information or fear of change.

The facilitator points out that sharing meaningful personal information in the form of a self-disclosure and listening to constructive responses from those who are trusted can lead to fewer "blind spots" and greater access to options that would otherwise remain unknown.

Inquiry

The facilitator guides the group sharing of information by adapting the questions and statements in the Activity Inquiry Fan to the content of this experience.

Samples:

Tell three things that you learned about others that you didn't know before.
Pretend that you are telling a friend about this experience. How would you explain it to them?
Name some trusted people with whom you would feel safe sharing personal information.

My Window[1]
Practice

Objective

Group members will interact to disclose personal information and listen to constructive responses to learn about possible "blind spots" and to discover knowledge previously unavailable to them.

Materials

"My Window" sheet (Experience 6.9), pencils, pens

Procedure

Group members are given the "My Window" sheet (Experience 6.9) and are divided into triads. These small groups are given the following instructions:

1. In the top left window, write down something everyone knows about you. Check this out with your group partners.
2. In the box beneath the first one, write a "secret" about yourself which you wouldn't mind sharing with the group. When this is done, share "secrets" in your triad.
3. In your small group, ask permission from group members to give others feedback about something you may know about them of which they may be unaware. Do this for everyone in the group in the form of a nature metaphor. Write down what others say in the top right window pane. For example, "Carl, may I share some information with you? When I watch you in group, I notice how carefully you choose your words. You remind me of a deer moving cautiously into a clearing in the woods."
4. Spend a few minutes alone and write down in the last empty window something important that you learned about yourself during this activity. For example: "I learned that I come across as being very cautious to others. I think that's because I'm always afraid that I will say something wrong and maybe get laughed at or rejected."

---

[1] Adapted from the Johari Window Model, Joseph Ingram and Harry Luft, as sited in *The 1973 Annual Handbook for Group Facilitators*, University Associates, 1973.)

Level I Variations:

The directions for younger and/or less mature groups could be presented as follows:

1. In the top left window, write or draw a picture of something everyone knows about you.

2. Use a slip of paper and write down or draw a picture of something that no one knows about you and that you wouldn't mind sharing. Put all of these "secrets" in the middle of the group. Choose one to share with the group and ask everyone to try and guess whose "secret" it is. Next, draw your "secret" in the bottom left pane of the My Window (Experience 6.9).

3. Ask for specific information about yourself from other group members. Write or draw something that is said in the top right window.
    Examples:
    "I want information about what is likeable about me."
    "Please tell me the best thing that I contribute to the group."

4. In the last empty box, write or draw the most important thing that you learned about yourself from the activity.

Inquiry

The facilitator guides the group sharing of information by adapting the questions and statements in the Activity Inquiry Fan to the content of this experience.

Samples:
How did it feel to participate in the experience?
How easy or hard was it to share a secret?
What did you learn about yourself and others that you didn't know before? How is it helpful to know this information now?

My Window

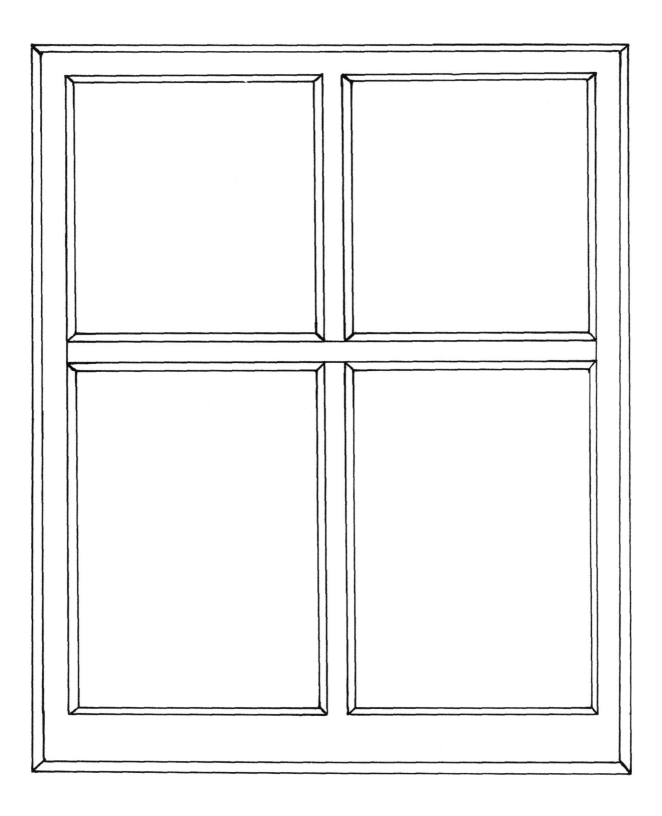

Secrets That I Keep
Transfer

Objective

Group members will record in their journals any "secrets" that they keep and will reflect on the possible benefits of sharing this information with people they trust.

Materials

Journals, colored pens

Procedure

Group members are asked to draw the outline of a human form to represent themselves. Inside the shape they are asked to draw a symbol for, or picture of, a secret they have. They are directed to draw this in the part of the body they imagine the secret is hidden i.e., in the heart, in the stomach, in the brain, or some other area. Each is asked to think about and/or write down the benefits of sharing the secret and getting information from others about it. They are asked to consider any fears they have about expressing the information to others. Members are also asked to list safe people and places for divulging the information.

The Communication Basics and In-depth Communication Tools acquired in this chapter are refined during subsequent group meetings. The communication focus in this section has been about listening to and expressing ideas and opinions. For many people, a more difficult task is attempting to communicate the feelings that are associated with thoughts and actions. The next series of experiences in *Chapter 7: Focusing on Feelings*, is designed to increase group members' comfort with human emotions as they learn to identify their own feelings, "read" the obvious and subtle emotional states expressed by others, develop an extensive vocabulary of feeling words, and learn to share their feelings effectively.

Facilitator Log

Things to remember:

_____

_____

_____

_____

_____

_____

_____

_____

_____

_____

_____

_____

_____

_____

_____

_____

_____

_____

_____

_____

_____

_____

_____

_____

_____

Focusing on Feelings

Chapter 7

Throughout the People Skills training, group members are given opportunities to practice "reading," labeling, "owning," and disclosing feelings, which are foundational tools of the Belonging Program. Each group session begins with a statement of how everyone is feeling. The emphasis placed on the ability to clearly express one's own feelings and interpret how others feel contributes greatly to each member's success with all other People Skills (e.g., disclosing strong feelings around a disappointment may reduce someone's need to act out, acknowledging the fact that one is nervous about making friends may ease a person's anxiety, letting people know positive feelings one has for them may increase cooperative interactions, and properly interpreting the feelings of others may lessen conflicts).

The following series of activities was selected to help people learn to "read" verbal and nonverbal cues in order to accurately label their own feelings and the feelings of others. The experiences also enable participants to practice how and when to express feelings using "I" statements. In addition, group members develop an expanded vocabulary of feeling words, which allows them to more accurately comprehend and express an array of emotions. The final set of activities in this section is designed to promote free, creative exploration of feelings. Through these expressive exercises, group members relax and experience emotions as "energy in motion" rather than something to be avoided, hidden, and/ or disowned.

Set I. Purpose:

To help group members identify and label how they and others are feeling by observing body language and listening for verbal clues

Emotional Postures
Awareness

Objective

Group members will identify and label feelings based on observation of body postures, movements and language.

Materials

None

Procedure

The facilitator asks group members to position themselves in the following manner. After each change of body posture, group members are asked to project how someone who sits or stands like that may be feeling and what s/he may be saying.

1. sit erect (proud)
2. sit slumped with head back and legs crossed (relaxed)
3. sit slumped with head down and hands folded (sad)
4. sit erect, pulling back with face covered (frightened)
5. stand erect with feet apart and arms folded (angry)
6. stand with legs apart and arms up in the air (surprised)
7. stand with arms pushing away (disgusted)
8. stand with head back and hand on chin (thoughtful)
9. sit slumped with arms crossed and tapping foot (mad)
10. stand with body completely limp (depressed)

Next, the facilitator asks groups members to demonstrate the following emotional postures and include words that they might be thinking or saying.

1. annoyed
2. cheerful
3. exhausted
4. fascinated
5. lonely
6. nervous
7. overwhelmed
8. shy
9. tense
10. fearful

Inquiry
The facilitator guides the group sharing of information by adapting the questions and statements in the Activity Inquiry Fan to the content of this experience.

Samples:
Which feelings were the hardest for you to identify and label? Which were the easiest?
What is the importance of learning to "read" body language and listen for clues about how someone is feeling?
Think of a situation from your past when you either read or misread the clues that told about how someone was feeling.

Alphabet of Emotions
Practice

Objective
Group members will practice identifying, labeling, "reading," and expressing feelings based upon body language and verbal clues.

Materials
Copies of the "Alphabet of Emotions" poster (Experience 7.1) for each group member, construction paper, markers, crayons, scissors, glue

Procedure
The facilitator provides a copy of the "Alphabet of Emotions" poster for each group member. Each person chooses a feeling from the poster and demonstrates it to the group using body posture, movement, and words. Others in the group try to guess the emotion being portrayed. Next, group members use the art supplies provided to create their personal "Alphabet of Emotions" poster by coloring the images, cutting them out, and pasting them onto construction paper. These are displayed in the group meeting room to be referenced at the beginning of each group session as members share a feeling sentence. At the end of a group's time together, the facilitator has the posters laminated for members to take home for continued use.

Inquiry
The facilitator guides the group sharing of information by adapting the questions and statements in the Activity Inquiry Fan to the content of this experience.

Samples:
Name one thing you liked about doing this activity?
Make up a new activity in which you could use the "Alphabet of Emotions" poster.
Explain why this activity has the title that it does.

Alphabet of Emotions

Abandoned	Amused	Brave	Bugged
Content	Crushed	Delighted	Depressed
Embarrassed	Enchanted	Fascinated	Frantic
Grateful	Grieved	Helpful	Hurt
Important	Infatuated	Jealous	Joyous
Kindhearted	Knowledgeable	Lonely	Loved

Mean	*Mellow*	*Needed*	*Numb*
Optimistic	*Outraged*	*Peaceful*	*Petrified*
Queasy	*Quiet*	*Refreshed*	*Rejected*
Shocked	*Sympathetic*	*Terrible*	*Thoughtful*
Uplifted	*Uptight*	*Violent*	*Vivacious*
Weary	*Wonderful*	*Yucky*	*Zippy*

Feelings Collage
More Practice

Objective

Group members will gain skill "reading" and labeling emotions by completing a cooperative feelings collage.

Materials

Magazines with pictures of people, "Alphabet of Emotions" (Experience 7.1), glue, butcher paper

Procedure

The facilitator directs group members to cut out pictures of people whose body language/facial expressions demonstrate a variety of feeling states. These are glued onto butcher paper until it is completely covered. Group members use the "Alphabet of Emotions" poster and take turns identifying the feelings represented in the collage. They are encouraged to use the "Alphabet of Emotions" poster to find synonyms for common feeling words. For example, angry could be irritated, aggravated, or furious.

Variation 1:

For a group of young children, the facilitator can label several feeling words on butcher paper (e.g., angry, excited, lonely, afraid), and ask the children to find pictures to illustrate those specific feeling words. They then glue the pictures next to the appropriate feeling word.

Variation 2:

Group members each have a shoe box, which they cover with magazine pictures depicting various emotions. On the outside of the box and lid, members paste pictures of feelings that they show easily to the rest of the world. On the inside of the box, group members create a collage of pictures that show the emotions that they keep hidden or private.

Inquiry

The facilitator guides the group sharing of information by adapting the questions and statements in the Activity Inquiry Fan to the content of this experience.

Samples:

Name two emotions that you express easily. Name two that are hard for you to show or talk about. Think about your friends. Name the emotion that you think they have the hardest time expressing or talking about. How did it feel to work together on this project?

Journal Writing: Body Language
Transfer

Objective

Group members will practice "reading" and labeling body language away from the group by completing a journal exercise.

Materials

Journals, pens

Procedure

Group members are asked to observe the people in their daily lives and write down examples of body language and verbal cues that helped them determine how those people were feeling during different daily experiences.

Set II. Purpose:

To help members accurately label feelings and expand their vocabulary of feeling words in order to become more emotionally literate

Feelings Brainstorm
Awareness

Objective

Group members will begin to expand their feelings' vocabulary by participating in a brainstorming session.

Materials

Butcher paper, felt pens

Procedure

The facilitator guides group members in a brainstorm of feeling words by giving the prompt "I feel _____" and asking them to fill in the blank with as many words as they can. The facilitator continues to prompt the group with such statements as "think of another word for that one" or "what's the opposite of that feeling?" The facilitator or a volunteer from the group records all of the words that are shared during the brainstorm. The list is kept for use in the next activity. Chart 7.2 contains a comprehensive listing of Feeling Words.

Inquiry

The facilitator guides the group sharing of information by adapting the questions and statements in the Activity Inquiry Fan to the content of this experience.

Samples:

How many feeling words are on our list? How many of these tell about upbeat feelings?

Tell about the three feelings on our list that you experience most often.

Name any feeling words that are new to you.

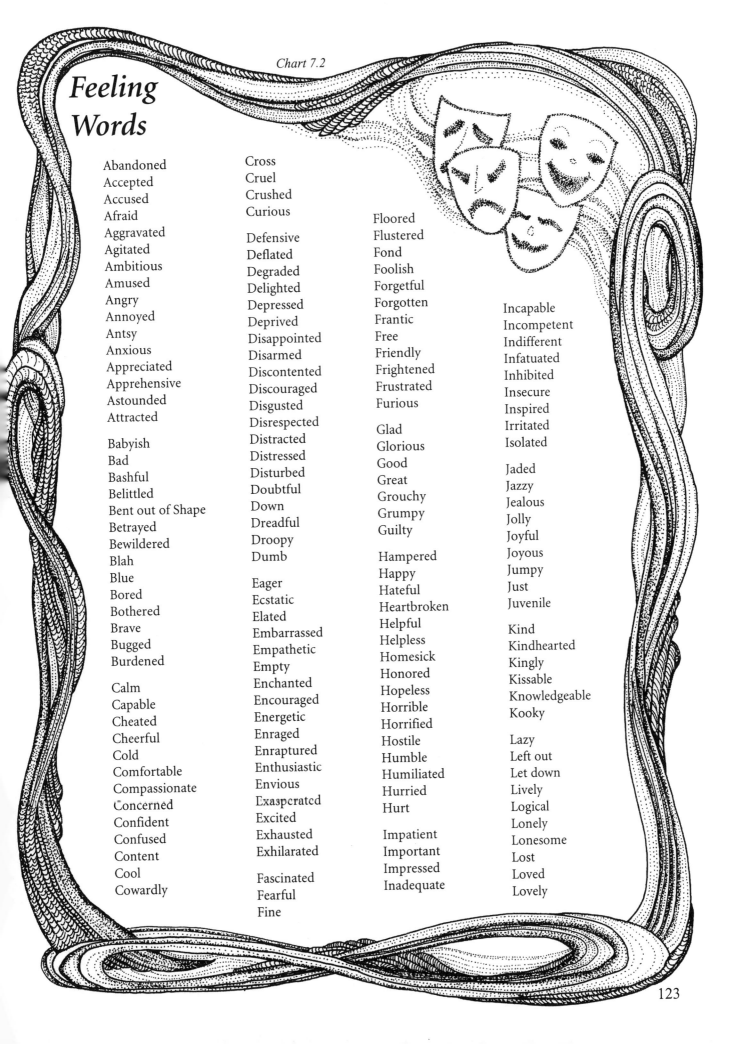

Feeling Words

Chart 7.2

Abandoned
Accepted
Accused
Afraid
Aggravated
Agitated
Ambitious
Amused
Angry
Annoyed
Antsy
Anxious
Appreciated
Apprehensive
Astounded
Attracted

Babyish
Bad
Bashful
Belittled
Bent out of Shape
Betrayed
Bewildered
Blah
Blue
Bored
Bothered
Brave
Bugged
Burdened

Calm
Capable
Cheated
Cheerful
Cold
Comfortable
Compassionate
Concerned
Confident
Confused
Content
Cool
Cowardly

Cross
Cruel
Crushed
Curious

Defensive
Deflated
Degraded
Delighted
Depressed
Deprived
Disappointed
Disarmed
Discontented
Discouraged
Disgusted
Disrespected
Distracted
Distressed
Disturbed
Doubtful
Down
Dreadful
Droopy
Dumb

Eager
Ecstatic
Elated
Embarrassed
Empathetic
Empty
Enchanted
Encouraged
Energetic
Enraged
Enraptured
Enthusiastic
Envious
Exasperated
Excited
Exhausted
Exhilarated

Fascinated
Fearful
Fine

Floored
Flustered
Fond
Foolish
Forgetful
Forgotten
Frantic
Free
Friendly
Frightened
Frustrated
Furious

Glad
Glorious
Good
Great
Grouchy
Grumpy
Guilty

Hampered
Happy
Hateful
Heartbroken
Helpful
Helpless
Homesick
Honored
Hopeless
Horrible
Horrified
Hostile
Humble
Humiliated
Hurried
Hurt

Impatient
Important
Impressed
Inadequate

Incapable
Incompetent
Indifferent
Infatuated
Inhibited
Insecure
Inspired
Irritated
Isolated

Jaded
Jazzy
Jealous
Jolly
Joyful
Joyous
Jumpy
Just
Juvenile

Kind
Kindhearted
Kingly
Kissable
Knowledgeable
Kooky

Lazy
Left out
Let down
Lively
Logical
Lonely
Lonesome
Lost
Loved
Lovely

123

Low
Loyal
Lucky

Mad
Magical
Magnificent
Marvelous
Maternal
Mature
Mean
Meek
Mellow
Mischievous
Miserable
Mixed-up
Modest

Nasty
Needed
Neighborly
Nervous
Nice
Noisy
Numb

Oblivious
Observant
Obstinate
Odd
Old
Opinionated
Optimistic
Ordinary
Ornery
Overwhelmed

Panicky
Paralyzed

Patient
Peaceful
Peculiar
Perplexed
Persecuted
Persistent
Perturbed
Pessimistic
Petrified
Picked-on
Playful
Pleasant
Pleased
Polite
Poor
Popular
Positive
Powerful
Pretty
Protective
Proud
Provoked
Put-down
Puzzled

Qualified
Quarrelsome
Queazy
Queenlike
Questionable
Quick
Quiet
Quizzical

Radiant
Reasonable
Rebellious
Refreshed
Regal
Rejected
Relaxed
Relieved

Reluctant
Remorseful
Resentful
Respected
Rested
Restless
Rich
Ridiculous
Romantic
Rude

Sad
Safe
Sarcastic
Satisfied
Scared
Self-conscious
Selfish
Sensitive
Serene
Serious
Shattered
Shocked
Shy
Silent
Silly
Simple
Sincere
Skeptical
Slow
Small
Smart
Sober
Sophisticated
Sorrowful
Sorry
Special
Startled
Sunny
Sympathetic

Talkative
Tall
Tearful
Tense
Terrible

Thoughtful
Thrilled
Ticked Off
Timid
Tired
Tough
Troubled
Trustworthy
Truthful
Turbulent

Ugly
Uncertain
Uneasy
Unhappy
Unique
Unsure
Unusual
Uptight
Uplifted
Upset
Used
Useful

Vague
Valuable
Violated
Violent
Vivacious
Volatile

Weak
Weary
Well
Wicked
Wild
Wise
Witty
Worried
Worthless

Young
Youthful
Yucky
Yummy

Zany
Zealous
Zippy

Chart of Emotions
Practice

Objective

Group members will brainstorm synonyms for common feeling words in order to increase their vocabulary of emotions.

Materials

"Chart of Emotions" drawn on butcher paper (see model below), the brainstorm list of feeling words from the previous session, felt markers

Procedure

One group member serves as a recorder. The others find words from the brainstorm list that are similar in meaning to the words at the top of each column on the continuum. These words are then recorded in the proper category. The list of feeling words on the "Alphabet of Emotions" poster (Experience 7.1) and Feeling Words (Experience 7.2) also can be used to assist the group in the activity. This Chart of Emotions, the brainstorm list, and "Alphabet of Emotions" poster are left on display in the group meeting room to help group members refine their use of feeling words.

Chart of Emotions			
Happy	Sad	Mad	Scared

Inquiry

The facilitator guides the group sharing of information by adapting the questions and statements in the Activity Inquiry Fan to the content of this experience.

Samples:

Name three happy feelings, sad feelings, mad feelings, and scared feelings.

Make up a new activity so that you could teach your friends this information.

Think of a life experience that you had today. How did you feel?

Journal Writing: Exploring Feelings
Transfer

Objective

Group members will demonstrate increased emotional literacy by completing an independent journal-writing exercise.

Materials

Journals, pens or pencils

Procedure

The facilitator asks group members to respond to the following prompt by writing or drawing in their journals:

"Choose a feeling word from those we have learned. Write or draw about a time when you felt that way."

Linda Lyon-Wright 1987

Set III. Purpose:

To help members communicate their emotions effectively and learn to take responsibility for their feelings

"I Feel ..." Statements
Awareness

Objective

Group members will complete and restate sentences to make "I feel ..." statements to gain awareness of how to effectively and responsibly communicate emotions.

Materials

Sentence examples (included below)

Procedure

The facilitator reads all group members a sentence and asks them to either complete it or restate it, using "I feel ..." as the opening. The progression of sentences given below moves from simple to complex in terms of the independent thinking required.

Level I

Complete the following statements:

1. When someone I like says hello to me, I feel _____.
2. When a friend asks me to play, I feel _____.
3. When I get money for doing a chore, I feel _____.
4. When I volunteer my time, I feel _____.
5. When I help a friend, I feel _____.
6. When I ask for help, I _____.
7. When I don't understand something, I _____.
8. When I like someone, and they don't like me, _____.
9. When a friend borrows something and doesn't return it, _____.
10. When I go somewhere I really like, _____.

Restate the following information, starting with "I feel ...":

1. I watched a scary movie last night.
2. My teacher never calls on me in class.
3. Grandma came to visit and brought me a surprise.
4. My class is going on a field trip tomorrow.
5. Doug and Shannon wouldn't let me play soccer with them at recess.
6. I twisted my ankle and fell in front of everyone.
7. I'm not allowed to play with my friend Kathy.
8. My bike is old and rusty.
9. David always finishes his work before I do.
10. My friend asked me to spend the night.

Level II

Complete the following statements:

1. When a stranger says hello to me, I feel _____ .
2. When someone I like asks me out, I feel _____ .
3. When I am earning money, I feel _____ .
4. When someone stares at me, I feel _____ .
5. When I help a friend, I feel _____ .
6. When I ask for help, I _____ .
7. When I don't understand something , I _____ .
8. When I like people, and they don't like me, _____ .
9. When a friend borrows my things and doesn't return them, _____ .
10. When I'm dressed up to go out, _____ .

Restate the following information, starting with "I feel …":

1. I went to a horror movie last weekend.
2. Mr. Brown always reads Carol's work to the class.
3. My grandmother took me shopping and bought me a lot of new clothes.
4. The French Club is going to Paris this spring.
5. I was eliminated from the basketball team.
6. I twisted my ankle and fell in front of everyone.
7. Jane's parents won't let us see each other.
8. This shirt is old and ugly.
9. Jack always finishes his exams before I do.
10. Paul held my hand on the way home.

Inquiry

The facilitator guides the group sharing of information by adapting the questions and statements in the Activity Inquiry Fan to the content of this experience.

Samples:

Name one thing in this activity that is about how people feel. Name one thing that is about how people act.
What do you think is the main point of this activity?
What do think it means to "own" your feelings?

Role-Playing Feelings
Practice

Objective

Group members will demonstrate ownership of their feelings by rephrasing sentences and making them "I feel ..." statements.

Materials

"Role-play Scripts" (Experiences 7.3 and 7.4)

Procedure

The facilitator reiterates that people often hide their feelings and/or pretend they belong to someone else by not claiming them with the simple word "I." Group members are given the following role-play situations. A pair acts out the script and then attempts to restructure the wording, using "I feel ..." statements. For example:

Jill: I've been curious about why you didn't try out for honor band.
Kim: Oh, it makes me too nervous to play alone in front of others.

Restated:
Jill: I've been curious about why you didn't try out for honor band.
Kim: Oh, I feel too nervous playing alone in front of others. I felt afraid to audition.

Inquiry

The facilitator guides the group sharing of information by adapting the questions and statements in the Activity Inquiry Fan to the content of this experience.

Samples:
How can you apply this skill in your daily life?
How would it benefit you and others if you used this skill in your daily life?
Why do you think that it is important to "own " your feelings?

Role-Play Scripts for "I Feel ..." Sentences
Level I

Scenario 1

Karen: What are you doing this weekend?

Sarah: My mom makes me so mad! She makes me do all of my chores before I can play.

Scenario 2

Jason: Do you want to come over and play Saturday?

Kerry: I get stuck doing the paper route with my brother on Saturdays. He aggravates me.

Scenario 3

Ted: What do you think of the new band instructor?

John: He makes me so embarrassed by having our section play alone.

Scenario 4

Kate: Why don't you ask the new girl to play basketball with us?

Bill: When she's around me, she makes me so shy I can't even say "Hi!"

Scenario 5

David: How did you do on the math test today?

Diane: Who knows! Ms. Kane makes me so nervous I can hardly add 2 + 2!

Scenario 6

Jesse: Are your parents sending you to camp this summer?

Mary: Are you kidding? They've got the stupid idea that kids should pay their own way!

Role-Play Scripts for "I Feel ..." Sentences
Level II

Scenario 1

Karen: What's everyone doing after the game tonight?

Sarah: My parents make me so mad. They're making me come home as soon as the game is over!

Scenario 2

Jason: Want to get together this weekend?

Kerry: That Jean! I get stuck going to the library with her every Saturday. She aggravates me.

Scenario 3

Ted: What do you think of the new band instructor?

John: He makes me so embarrassed by having our section play alone.

Scenario 4

Kate: Why don't you ask him to the dance?

Cindy: No way! When he's around me, I can't even say "Hi!"

Scenario 5

David: How did you do on the math test today?

Diane: Who knows! Ms. Kane makes me so nervous I can hardly add 2 + 2!

Scenario 6

Jesse: Are your parents going to lend you the money for the ski trip?

Mary: When you have to work every weekend for a month to get one stupid ski trip, it makes you pretty mad!

Owning My Feelings
More Practice

Objective
Group members will become more skilled at using "I feel …" statements to demonstrate that they are taking responsibility for their own feelings.

Materials
"Owning My Feelings" (Experience 7.5), pens or pencils

Procedure
The facilitator gives each member a copy of the "Owning My Feelings" sheet (Experience 7.4). On the sheet are examples of statements in which feelings aren't "owned" by the speaker. Group members are asked to rewrite or retell the sentences so that the speaker takes responsibility for what is being said by starting each sentence with "I feel …", "I felt …" or "I am feeling …".

Example: Everyone teases me about how curly my hair is. Some people hate to be teased.

Restate: I feel frustrated and embarrassed when people tease me about my curly hair.

Inquiry
The facilitator guides the group sharing of information by adapting the questions and statements in the Activity Inquiry Fan to the content of this experience.

Samples:

What did we just do in this activity?

How does it feel to take responsibility for your feelings?

How could you apply this skill in your own life?

Journal Writing: "I Feel …"
Transfer

Objective
Group members will apply the newly learned skill of using "I feel …" statements in their daily lives.

Materials
Journals, pens or pencils

Procedure
The facilitator asks group members to record three times that they were able to use an "I feel …" statement in their day-to-day experiences with family and friends.

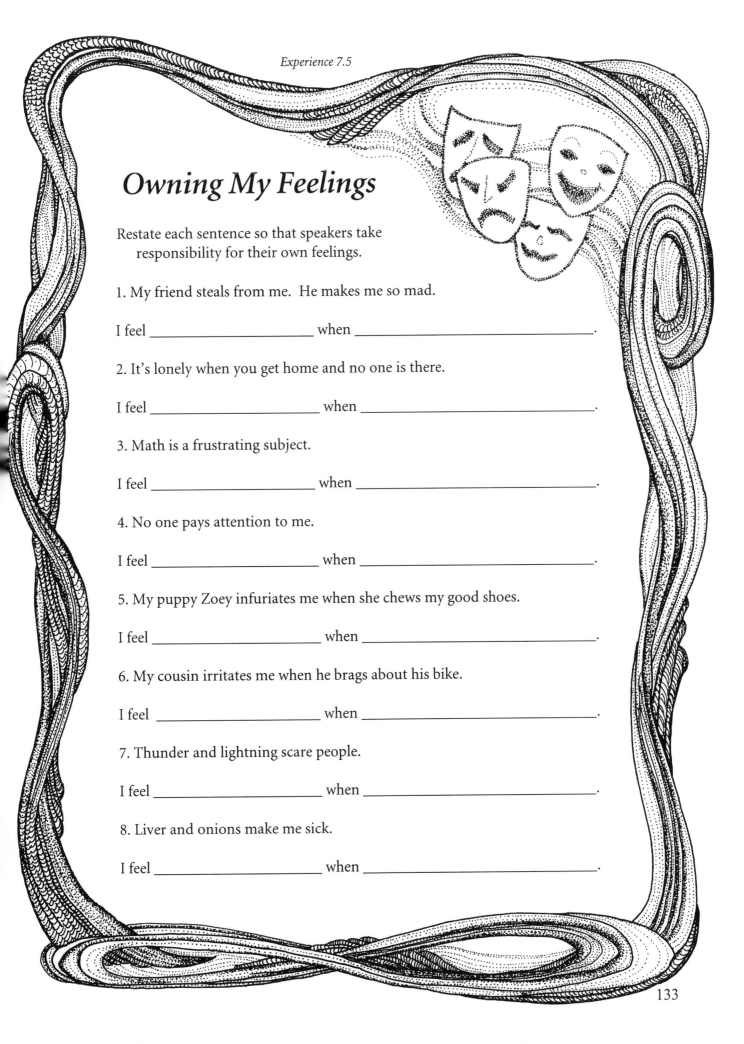

Owning My Feelings

Restate each sentence so that speakers take
responsibility for their own feelings.

1. My friend steals from me. He makes me so mad.

I feel _____ when _____.

2. It's lonely when you get home and no one is there.

I feel _____ when _____.

3. Math is a frustrating subject.

I feel _____ when _____.

4. No one pays attention to me.

I feel _____ when _____.

5. My puppy Zoey infuriates me when she chews my good shoes.

I feel _____ when _____.

6. My cousin irritates me when he brags about his bike.

I feel _____ when _____.

7. Thunder and lightning scare people.

I feel _____ when _____.

8. Liver and onions make me sick.

I feel _____ when _____.

Set IV. Purpose:

To provide opportunities for group members to become comfortable with their feelings through creative expression

Feeling Color Wheel
Awareness

Objective

Group members will expand their ability to express feelings freely and comfortably by completing a color association activity.

Materials

"Feeling Color Wheel" (Experience 7.6), crayons, colored chalk or pencils

Procedure

The facilitator passes out the "Feeling Color Wheel" and leads a discussion, reviewing the common feeling/color associations listed below. Members are encouraged to create their own feeling-color connections, as well. It is helpful for them to make a key of the feeling words and colors used to represent them on the bottom of the page.

Common Feeling-Color Associations
   red - anger
   blue - sad/sorrow
   white - hope
   pink - happy/healthy
   green - envy
   black - depression
   yellow - cheerful

Inquiry

The facilitator guides the group sharing of information by adapting the questions and statements in the Activity Inquiry Fan to the content of this experience.

Samples:
What is one thing you learned in this activity?
Can you think of another name for this activity?
What part of this activity was the most difficult for you?

Feeling Color Wheel

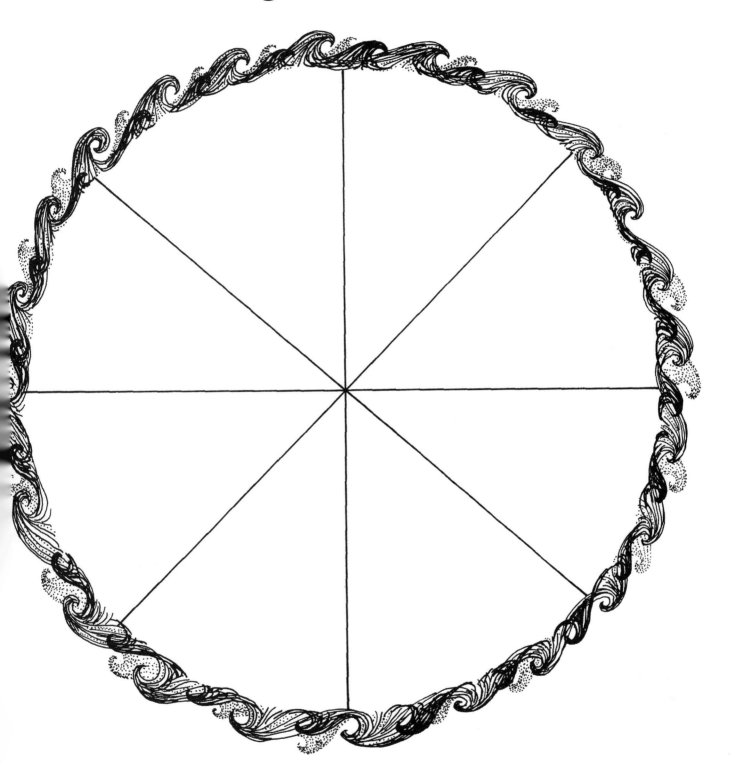

Heart Colors
Practice

Objective
Group members will explore their emotions through the use of color and symbols.

Materials
Drawing paper, crayons or pens

Procedure
The facilitator leads a discussion about how feelings are often associated with the heart (e.g., the heart shape is a traditional symbol of love and affection). We say things like "My heart is full of sadness," "I'm heartbroken," or "I feel joy in my heart." The discussion then moves to include feeling-color associations. For example, the color red is frequently associated with anger, blue with sorrow, green with envy, and black with depression. Next, group members draw large heart shapes and use colors to depict the variety of feelings that they have in their heart. Members identify feeling words they associate with a given color and tell why, whenever possible. It can be helpful for members to create a color key on their drawing to note which feeling they are associating with which color. There are no right or wrong answers.

Variation:
Group members draw two, large, identically shaped hearts on white butcher paper. Each person uses tempera paints to add colors that depict their feelings to both of the hearts. When the paint is dry, they cut out the hearts, place them back-to-back, and stuff them with crumpled paper while stapling the hearts together. Strings are added so that they can be hung from the ceiling.

Inquiry
The facilitator guides the group sharing of information by adapting the questions and statements in the Activity Inquiry Fan to the content of this experience.

Samples:
What was the most significant part of this activity for you?
How did you feel at the beginning, middle, and end of this activity?
Would you recommend this activity to another group? Why?

Paint Your Feelings
More Practice

Objective

Group members will gain comfort with expressing their feelings by painting abstract pictures to represent different feeling states.

Materials

Paper, watercolors, quiet music, "Alphabet of Emotions" poster (Experience 7.1)

Procedure

Group members are given paper and watercolors and asked to choose a feeling or series of feeling words from the "Alphabet of Emotions" poster. With quiet music in the background, participants paint colors and abstract shapes to represent a particular feeling(s). Group members paint as many pictures as time allows. The pictures are then shared with the group. Members explain their choice of colors and symbols used to depict the chosen feeling(s).

Inquiry

The facilitator guides the group sharing of information by adapting the questions and statements in the Activity Inquiry Fan to the content of this experience.

Samples:
What is the value of this type of creative expression?
Pretend you are talking to your friends. Explain what we did in group today.
What was your favorite color to work with today? What feeling did it represent?

Journal Writing: Heart Drawings
Transfer

Objective

Group members will apply their ability to identify and express emotions by completing an independent journal writing/drawing exercise.

Materials

Journals, pens, watercolors

Procedure

Group members are asked to draw a heart shape in their journal for each day of the upcoming week. They are asked to color in or paint one heart daily, with a color that represents the most prominent feeling(s) they experienced on that particular day. They may choose to write about their feelings, as well.

As stated at the beginning of this chapter, being able to "read," label, "own," and express feelings are foundational tools of the Belonging Program. As group members become emotionally literate, they add one of the most significant competencies to their repertoire of People Skills. All of the skills practiced through the self-exploration and communication exercises of the previous three chapters are needed to form and maintain successful relationships, the theme of the next two chapters: *Chapter 8: Making Friends* and *Chapter 9: Cooperating With Others*.

Facilitator Log

Things to remember:

_____

_____

_____

_____

_____

_____

_____

_____

_____

_____

_____

_____

_____

_____

_____

_____

_____

_____

_____

_____

_____

Making Friends

Linda Lyon-Wright 1987

Chapter 8

Throughout the People Skills experiences practiced so far in *Belonging,* participants have gained a greater sense of self-worth and have worked to expand their repertoire of communication skills, both with ideas and emotions. These skills are called upon in this section as group members are guided through activities to help them form and maintain friendships with others. Participants begin by learning strategies to overcome fears or inhibitions that may keep them from having meaningful relationships. They are guided to understand that to have friends, people must first be a friend to themselves; they must like themselves. Next, the group considers those qualities and actions required to make and maintain healthy relationships with their friends. Finally, the group addresses the changing nature of relationships, as members are guided to recognize the rewards of their interactions with others, whether a friendship is short or long-lived.

Set I. Purpose:

To assist group members to overcome fears and inhibitions they may hold related to forming and maintaining relationships with others

Body Talk
Awareness

Objective

Group members will engage in conversation with themselves in order to become aware of fears that may inhibit their ability to form and maintain friendships.

Materials

Butcher paper, markers, pencils, pens

Procedure

The facilitator asks for a volunteer who, lies on a large piece of butcher paper and has his or her body outline drawn by another group member. Group members then write the following statements across the area of the body where each of the noted body parts is located:

Stomach: "When I meet new people, I get all knotted up."

Heart: "I start pounding when I call someone I like on the phone."

Hands: "I sweat whenever someone introduces me to a new person."

Throat: "Words get stuck in me when I try to talk to a new acquaintance."

Mouth: "I go dry when I'm trying to have a conversation with someone I like."

Eyes: "I really try to look at someone I am interested in knowing, but it's hard when they look right back at me."

Brain: "I just go dead when I try to think of things to say to new people I'd like to get to know."

Ears: "I turn bright red and burn when I'm with someone I want to get to know."

Skin: "I get so hot and flushed with embarrassment that I'm sure everyone notices."

Next, group members "ask" each body part the following question. Someone records the answers on the body poster.

"(Stomach, Heart, Hands, Throat, Mouth, Eyes, Brain), what are you afraid will happen when you meet someone you'd like to get to know better?"

After recording these fears, group members brainstorm suggestions for overcoming them and record these ideas on the group body poster.

Examples:

Stomach: "You could take slow, deep breaths to help you relax."

Heart: "You could think about all the wonderful qualities you have to bring to a friendship."

Hands: "You could hold yourselves together while you greet the new person."

Throat: "You could swallow hard and ask the new person a question to start the conversation."

Mouth: "You could tell the other person that you're really thirsty and invite them to go for a cold drink with you."

Eyes: "You could invite them to do something, like take a walk, so that you don't have to look directly at each other all of the time."

Brain: "You could give yourself a pep talk before meeting the person you want to get to know. Remind yourself that you are a worthwhile person with lots to share with others."

Ears: "You could listen to what your heart is saying about really wanting a friend and ignore how red you are."

Skin: "You could simply tell the people you are meeting that you always get nervous in new situations and are quite sure that you're bright red right now. Laugh about it with them."

The poster is saved for use throughout the activities in this chapter.

Inquiry

The facilitator guides the group sharing of information by adapting the questions and statements in the Activity Inquiry Fan to the content of this experience.

Samples:

What is the main point of this activity?

How did you feel at the beginning, middle, and end of this experience?

Think of a situation from your past. How could you handle it differently now that you have this information?

Interview: Friends and Me
Practice

Objective

Group members will gain confidence in their ability to overcome inhibitions so they are able to make friends.

Materials

"Interview-Friends and Me" (Experience 8.1), pencils

Procedure

The facilitator displays the group body poster from the previous experience for reference as group members move to quiet, private corners and ask themselves the questions on the "Interview: Friends and Me" sheet (Experience 8.1). The group rejoins to share results after five to eight minutes.

Inquiry

The facilitator guides the group sharing of information by adapting the questions and statements in the Activity Inquiry Fan to the content of this experience.

Samples:

Name three strategies that you learned to help you make new friends.

How could you apply what you have learned in this activity to your daily life?

Name one thing in this activity that was about how people feel. Name one thing in this activity that was about how people act.

Interview: Friends and Me

What is your full name ? _____

Tell about friends that you have or used to have. _____

_____

_____

_____

What makes you a good friend? _____

_____

_____

_____

Describe how you met and became close friends with someone._____

_____

_____

_____

How does your body react when you meet somebody new? _____

_____

_____

_____

What strategies do you now know that will make it easier to meet someone?_____

_____

_____

_____

Journal Writing: Letter Exchange
Transfer

Objective

Group members will demonstrate knowledge of how to overcome inhibitions that keep them from having friendships.

Materials

Journals, pencils, pens

Procedure

Group members are asked to write a brief letter to themselves in their journals. The letter starts with how they feel about that day in relationship to people they met or spent time with. They are asked to reflect upon how their body felt during the day. For example:

Dear Self,

I'm pretty happy today. I actually talked to Sarah. She's really easy to be with. My stomach hurt at first, but then we just had fun together, and I forgot about it.

Love,
Susan

Next , members are asked to write a response to the letter.

Dear Susan,

I'm happy when you're happy. I'm always reminding you how smart you are and how much fun you are. I'm not surprised that Sarah liked you right away. Maybe someday your stomach won't act up, but for now it's great that you just relax with the knots and go on and meet new people anyway.

Love,
Your Self

Set II. Purpose:

To guide group members toward an understanding of the qualities and actions necessary to make and keep friends

Be a Friend, Have a Friend
Awareness

Objective

Group members will gain an awareness of qualities and actions desired to be a friend and receive friendship from others.

Materials

"Be a Friend, Have a Friend" (Experience 8.2), pens or pencils

Procedure

The facilitator passes out the activity sheet, "Be a Friend, Have a Friend"(Experience 8.2) and asks group members to circle in red the qualities and actions of a good friend that they exhibit most of the time. Next, they circle in blue those qualities and actions that they exhibit only some of the time, if ever. These sheets are collected and saved for use in the next two practice experiences.

Inquiry

The facilitator guides the group sharing of information by adapting the questions and statements in the Activity Inquiry Fan to the content of this experience.

Samples:
Which friendship qualities would be most helpful in making and keeping friendships?
Which friendship qualities do you wish you could develop?
What positive actions are the easiest for you? Which are the hardest?

Be a Friend, Have a Friend

Friendship Qualities

Circle in red all of the friendship qualities you show most of the time.
Circle in blue the friendship qualities you show some of the time.

dependable	punctual	honest
polite	cheerful	helpful
cooperative	kind	neat
likeable	flexible	accepting
energetic	giving	respectful
understanding	trusting	loyal
humorous	gentle	forgiving
fair	careful	loving

Friendly Actions

Circle in red all the friendly actions you demonstrate to others most of the time.
Circle in blue all the friendly actions you demonstrate to others some of the time.

listen attentively when a friend is talking

provide support when a friend needs help with a problem

encourage others by giving compliments

share with others

say "I'm sorry" when it's needed

offer helpful suggestions when asked

take responsibility for yourself instead of blaming others

volunteer your time to help others

express gratitude, say "thanks"

make your friends a priority in your life

Turtle Talk
Practice

Objective
Group members will gain awareness of the qualities and actions necessary to make and maintain friendships.

Materials
"Be a Friend, Have a Friend" (Experience 8.2, completed in the previous session),
"Turtle Talk" (Experience 8.3), colored pens

Procedure
The facilitator passes out the "Be a Friend, Have a Friend" sheet (Experience 8.2) completed in the previous exercise. Group members refer to them as they complete "Turtle Talk" (Experience 8.3). Group members are given copies of "Turtle Talk" and are asked to write their names in the center of the turtle picture (Experience 8.3). In each of the sections of the turtle shell, members write or draw the following information:

1. three things that you do well
2. three ways that you help others
3. positive qualities that you bring to a friendship
4. three words that describe a close friend
5. three friendly things that others do for you
6. positive qualities that you'd like to develop

Group members are encouraged to decorate their turtles in unique ways. When all turtle drawings are completed and decorated, members choose a partner. Each pair talks about the drawings done by each person for three to five minutes. The listener in the pair is encouraged to ask questions.

Inquiry
The facilitator guides the group sharing of information by adapting the questions and statements in the Activity Inquiry Fan to the content of this experience.

Samples:
What did you learn about your partner that makes him or her a good friend?
What qualities are you and your partner going to develop? How will you do this?
What does this activity have to do with "give and take" in friendship?

Turtle Talk

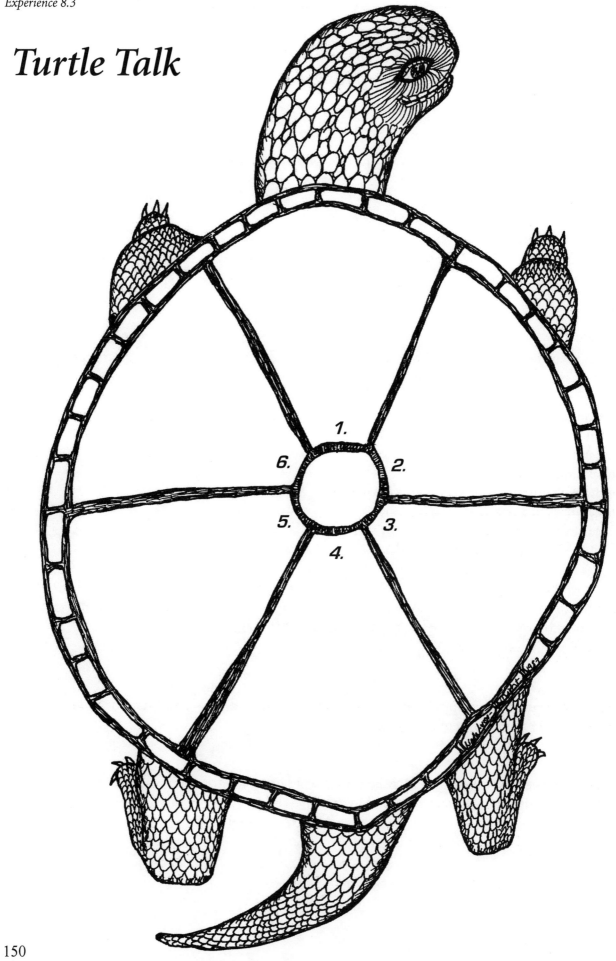

Improvement Plan
More Practice

Objective

Group members will acquire new friendship qualities and express them in the form of friendly actions toward others through the use of an improvement plan.

Materials

"Be a Friend, Have a Friend (Experience 8.2, completed previously), "Improvement Plan" (Experience 8.4), pencils or pens

Procedure

The facilitator provides each group member with their copy of "Be a Friend, Have a Friend" (Experience 8.2) which was completed previously and an "Improvement Plan" (Experience 8.4). Group members use the list of qualities and actions from experience 8.2 to stimulate discussion of the qualities each needs to develop or improve upon to be a good friend. Members choose one quality to improve upon and write it in the blank at the top of their Improvement Plan. Next, members select friendly actions that would demonstrate the friendship qualities that they are developing. They use the actions listed in Experience 8.2 and/or come up with specific ones of their own with the group's help. For example:

Quality to Develop: Being Forgiving
Actions:
- Listen to the reasons my friend gives for what she does.
- Tell my friend that I accept her apology when she says, "I'm sorry."
- Let my friends do things without me sometimes without getting mad at them.

Next group members complete the other two boxes on the Improvement Plan by selecting two additional qualities to work on expressing through friendly actions.

Inquiry

The facilitator guides the group sharing of information by adapting the questions and statements in the Activity Inquiry Fan to the content of this experience.

Samples:
How could you have used this information about being and having friends last year?
Name two things in this activity that are about how people act and two things about how people appear to be to others.
Tell about someone else's Improvement Plan.

Improvement Plan

Quality to Develop: _____

Actions:
  1)

  2)

  3)

Quality to Develop: _____

Actions:
  1)

  2)

  3)

Quality to Develop: _____

Actions:
  1)

  2)

  3)

Journal Writing: Progress Chart
Transfer

Objective

Group members will increase the number of friendship qualities and friendly actions they currently express by tracking their progress.

Materials

Journals, pens, pencils

Procedure

Group members are asked to track their progress with one or more of the qualities that they are working on by making a simple chart in their journals, as follows:

Quality to Develop:							
Actions	SU	M	T	W	TH	F	S
1.							
2.							
3.							

Each day of the week, group members put a check by the actions that they demonstrated on that particular day. They are encouraged to share what they are doing with trusted people in their lives (e.g., teacher, parent, group facilitator, another group member, coach, counselor, etc.).

Set III. Purpose:
To help group members understand changes in friendships: losing old friends and finding new ones

My Friends and I
Awareness

Objective
Group members will gain awareness of behaviors that support friendships and those that may lead to loss of friendships.

Materials
Nerf or other soft ball, "My Friends and I Situation Cards" (Experience 8.5)

Procedure
Group members are asked to sit in a circle. The situation cards are given out until all are used. Some members may have more than one card. The facilitator brings the nerf ball to the group and group members toss it freely around the circle. When the ball is thrown to the person with card #1, that person acts out what the card says using the ball. The action is then stopped and a discussion ensues about the action and how it relates to making and keeping friends. The following Inquiry statements and questions can be used by the facilitator after each ball toss situation.
- What does this behavior tell you about a person?
- What could you expect if you were friends with a person who behaved in this manner?
- How did it feel when the ball was passed in the way that it was? Would this action help someone make and keep friends? Why or why not?

After the discussion, the ball is again thrown freely back and forth among members until the person holding card #2 catches it. The Procedure continues until all eight cards have been used.

Inquiry
The facilitator guides the group sharing of information by adapting the questions and statements in the Activity Inquiry Fan to the content of this experience.

Samples:
What was the most challenging part of this activity?
Tell about how your feelings changed during different parts of this activity.
Think of a situation from your own life. How could you handle it differently now that you have this information?

My Friends and I Situation Cards

1. Hold the ball and throw it up and down in the air.

Don't pass it on to anyone else.

5. Point to one other person.

Throw the ball back and forth between the two of you, ignoring the others.

2. Indicate by pointing that the ball must go from person to person around the circle.

6. Pass the ball to someone else. Motion for him/her to pass it on to someone else.

When that person passes it on, reach over and grab the ball.

3. Point to two other people.

Indicate that the ball will only be thrown among the three of you.

7. Pass the ball to someone and indicate that it must come back to you.

Each person you throw to must return the ball to you. You are the only one who can pass the ball to a new person.

4. Hold the ball. Then throw it over your head so that it lands behind you, outside of the group.

8. Hold the ball. Slowly look at each person.

After you have had eye contact with everyone, carefully select someone and throw the ball to that member.

Good Friend Wanted
Practice

Objective

Group members will define qualities they desire in a friend as a means of helping them find new friends.

Materials

Blank paper, "Be a Friend, Have a Friend" (Experience 8.2) marking pens, crayons

Procedure

The facilitator passes out blank sheets of paper and asks group members to create a "Good Friend Wanted" Poster. Members may want to discuss the Friendship Qualities and Friendly Actions that they have learned in the past activities by referring to "Be a Friend, Have a Friend" (Experience 8.2) before developing their Wanted Posters. When everyone is finished, group members share what they have written about the new friend they would like to find.

Variation:

Group members create another poster entitled, "Friend Offered," to reinforce that to have a friend they must first be one.

Inquiry

The facilitator guides the group sharing of information by adapting the questions and statements in the Activity Inquiry Fan to the content of this experience.

Samples:

How were peoples' Wanted Posters the same? How were they different?
Name one thing in this activity that is about how people feel and one thing about how they act.
Why do you think it is important to ask for what you want in a friend?

Journal Writing: Golden Friends
Transfer

Objective
Group members will recall the benefits gained from past or longtime friendships.

Materials
Journals, pens

Procedure
The facilitator asks group members to reflect on the old adage: "Make new friends, but keep the old. One is silver and the other gold."

Then, group members are asked to find a quiet space and time during the week to remember old friends or friends that they have known for a very long time. It is suggested that they write a letter or write an imaginary phone conversation with one or more of these people in their journals. They are asked to share (1) what they most appreciate about the person(s), (2) how they feel about their friendship, and (3) how they have benefited from the relationship.

The activities in Chapter 8: Making Friends required that group members apply the People Skills learned to date as they consider themselves in relationship to other people—in this case, friends. In Chapter 9: Cooperating with Others, the group will explore behaviors needed to successfully work, play, or just be together with larger groups of people. It will also address the frustrations and the benefits of joining together with others in cooperative pursuits.

Facilitator Log

Things to remember:

158

Cooperating with Others

Chapter 9

For many group members, the support group experiences they are having while learning new People Skills represent their first successful attempts at belonging to a group. The series of activities in this chapter is sequential in nature, taking participants from working together with one or two people to participating in increasingly larger groups. The intent is to demonstrate behaviors required to successfully integrate into a desired group and maintain a position of acceptance. Group members focus on feelings associated with being part of a unit. Some advantages of successful working, playing, and being together, (e.g., cooperating with others) are explored.

Set I. Purpose:

To provide opportunities for group members to successfully cooperate with one other person and recognize the benefits of doing so

Mirror Images
Awareness

Objective

Group members will gain an awareness of how paying close attention to others is a required component of a successful cooperative endeavor.

Materials

None

Procedure

Divide group members into pairs. Initially, one person leads and the other imitates the leader's movements. Roles are then switched so each has a chance to lead and to follow. Eventually, no one leads and both partners contribute to the motion. Partners look each other in the eye and have slow, smooth, flowing motions. They will recognize after beginning to move together that quick, abrupt movements are difficult to follow. New partnerships can be formed as time allows.

Inquiry

The facilitator guides the group sharing of information by adapting the questions and statements in the Activity Inquiry Fan to the content of this experience.

Samples:

What did you and your partner have to do to be able to move as one?
How did it feel when you both began to move as one?
What was the easiest part of this experience? What was the hardest?

Cooperative Drawings
Practice

Objective

Group members will gain experience with behaviors required for a successful cooperative effort.

Materials

Construction paper, crayons, colored pencils, felt pens

Additional materials for variations: finger paints, clay, play dough, glue, glitter, magazine pictures, popsicle sticks, pipe cleaners, buttons, etc.

Procedure

The facilitator explains to the group that each member will have a partner and jointly draw a picture. Group members either choose a partner or are randomly assigned one. The dynamics of the experience are frequently very different, depending upon whether or not members choose to work together. All persons have an opportunity to draw something on their own sides of the paper. The pair then draws something together in the middle of the page. The center drawing is something mutually agreed upon and drawn (see diagram suggestions below). Members are encouraged to have a planning discussion before drawing. Both people must be in agreement before beginning to create the product. The facilitator leads a follow-up brainstorming activity and lists all of the behaviors given as being examples of cooperation. This list is posted to help group members evaluate future cooperative experiences.

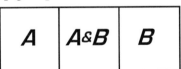 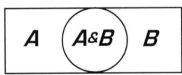

Variation 1: The facilitator instructs group members to complete another cooperative drawing, but to do so without talking. Members choose their partners or are randomly paired by the facilitator. Each pair is given a blank sheet of paper to share. Partners complete a single cooperative picture without talking and without dividing the paper in any way. They may use hand signals, facial expressions, or other body language to communicate about their product.

Variation 2: Group members select partners or are randomly assigned one. The partners agree on a single drawing, painting, or construction project to be created by both. One person draws or makes the first part of the project, working for about one minute. The next person contributes something to the creation and returns it to the first person to add on another part, and so on. Finger paints, clay, and/or assorted materials for collage making add interest to the activity.

Inquiry

The facilitator guides the group sharing of information by adapting the questions and statements in the Activity Inquiry Fan to the content of this experience.

Samples:

How did you feel while you were doing this activity? How did you feel about your finished project?

Name three advantages of working with someone else. Name any disadvantages.

What did you and your partner do that showed that you were cooperating?

What were the easiest things for you to do? What were the hardest?

Journal Writing: Cooperative Survey
Transfer

Objective

Group members will apply their knowledge of cooperative behaviors by noting examples of them in their daily lives.

Materials

Journals, pens, and pencils

Procedure

The facilitator asks group members to make note of one example of cooperation they observe on each day of the upcoming week and write these instances in their journals. Group members are guided to watch for cooperative actions in their family, at school, in restaurants or stores, and/or during sports or other activity practices.

Set II. Purpose:

To provide opportunities for group members to participate successfully in cooperative group experiences involving two or more other people

People Machines
Awareness

Objective

Group members will gain an awareness of additional behaviors needed to have a successful cooperative interaction with two or more individuals.

Materials

None

Procedure

Members are divided into groups of two to four. The facilitator explains that each group will figure out a way to move and/or hold their bodies to create some type of a machine. The facilitator asks a group of volunteers to demonstrate the idea by creating a washing machine. Two people hold hands with outstretched arms. The third person stands between the others and moves around as the "laundry." Other possibilities include a motorcycle, car, video game, or computer.

Members are given several minutes to create one of the above-mentioned machines or one of their own choice. The machines are demonstrated to the rest of the group. Everyone tries to guess what the machine is.

Variation: Groups create "imaginary machines," as opposed to something that everyone would recognize. Members of a group of two to four people take time to build and rehearse their "machines" before demonstrating them. Others think of names and functions for the imaginary machines.

Inquiry

The facilitator guides the group sharing of information by adapting the questions and statements in the Activity Inquiry Fan to the content of this experience.

Samples:
Describe how different people contributed to the creation of the machine.
What did you discover about how you cooperate with others?
What was the hardest part of this activity for you? the funniest? the easiest?

Group Puzzle Pictures
Practice

Objective

Group members will practice cooperative behaviors to successfully complete a project with small groups of three to five other people.

Materials

11x17 white construction paper cut into four to six odd-shaped pieces, crayons, colored pens or pencils, tape, the list of cooperative behaviors from the previous Cooperative Drawing activity (page 163).

Procedure

Groups of three or four are formed either by self-selection (who would like to work with whom) or random selection (putting names in a hat and drawing out three or four). Each group is given a set of puzzle pieces with the same number of pieces as there are people in the group. When these pieces are taped together, they will form an 11x17 sheet. To help group members assemble the pieces, the facilitator marks the backside of each puzzle piece with a dot or a check mark.

Participants work together to assemble the puzzle pieces and tape them together to reconstruct the 11x17 sheet of blank paper. Next, they decide on a theme for a picture, and each member contributes by drawing a part of the picture. While this process is unfolding, the facilitator points out examples of cooperative behaviors that are being demonstrated, refers people to the posted list of cooperative behaviors for guidance, helps mediate conflicts, and makes suggestions if a group "gets stuck."

Inquiry

The facilitator guides the group sharing of information by adapting the questions and statements in the Activity Inquiry Fan to the content of this experience.

Samples:

How did the group work together? What did you contribute?
How did you feel at the beginning, middle, and end of this activity?
What do you think is the main point of all of these cooperative experiences?

Odds and Ends Sculpture
More Practice

Objective

Group members will practice cooperative behaviors required to successfully complete a project with a small group of three to five other people.

Materials

Paper scraps, cans, pipe cleaners, popsicle sticks, glue, stapler, scissors, tape, glitter, styrofoam balls and packing pellets, buttons, boxes, cardboard tubes, egg cartons, other small items

Procedure

The facilitator explains to the group(s) that they will be making a cooperative sculpture with a name such as "Clunko," "Tiptover,"or "Ginjac." (The facilitator suggests a name or asks the group to make up a name.) Groups of three to five are formed by self or random selection. Each group is given a similar set of odds and ends and is instructed to work together to create a single sculpture. Members are encouraged to use their creativity. They are asked to talk about and plan the sculpture before starting and throughout its creation. The facilitator indicates that everyone needs to contribute something to the final creation. When the sculptures are finished, the facilitator asks group members to talk about their creation, sharing its name, what it likes to do, where it lives, how it acts, or any other information they would like to provide.

Inquiry

The facilitator guides the group sharing of information by adapting the questions and statements in the Activity Inquiry Fan to the content of this experience.

Samples:

Name three things that helped your group complete the project. Name three things that hindered that process.
How did your group decide what to make?
How is the group sculpture different than it would have been if you had done it alone?

Journal Writing: Cooperating at Home
Transfer

Objective

Group members will apply their knowledge of cooperative behaviors to their home lives.

Materials

Journals, pencils or pens

Procedure

Members are asked to write in their journals about ways that they cooperate at home, particularly in relation to family tasks such as:
1. cleaning the house
2. preparing meals
3. helping with younger siblings
4. getting ready for a trip or vacation
5. resolving a conflict

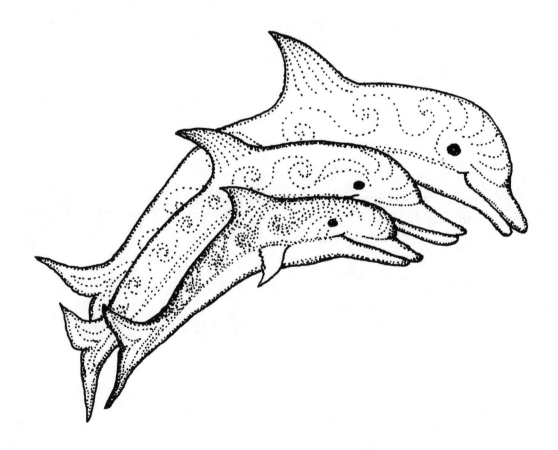

Set III. Purpose:

To provide members with the information and skills required to actively participate in large groups

Knot Game
Awareness

Objective

Group members will gain an awareness of the behaviors required to have a successful cooperative experience with larger groups of people.

Materials

An open space

Procedure

Group members, including the facilitator, hold hands and form a large circle. People then begin to form a knot by tangling, twisting, turning, and stepping over others, without dropping hands. Once this knot of people is created, the group works together to untangle itself back into the orginal circle. Group members are encouraged to offer suggestions to each other to help the group work.

Inquiry

The facilitator guides the group sharing of information by adapting the questions and statements in the Activity Inquiry Fan to the content of this experience.

Samples:

Talk about how the group worked together during this activity.
How did your feelings change throughout the process of tangling and untangling?
Name one thing that you liked about doing this activity with others and one thing that you really didn't like.

Five Squares—Six-Inch Puzzle
Practice

Objective

Group members will practice cooperative behaviors required to complete a project with a larger number of people.

Materials

"Five Squares—Six-Inch Puzzle" sheet (Experience 9.1), previously cut into pieces by the facilitator

Procedure

This activity requires a group of five people. If there are extra people they assist the facilitator. If there are not enough people, the facilitator joins to make the required five. The facilitator indicates to group members that the goal of the exercise is for each player to form one six-inch square and draws an example of what a six-inch square will look like.

Groups of five people sit around a table or other hard surface. The facilitator carefully explains the ground rules for the activity before passing out the puzzle pieces. They are as follows:

Ground Rules:
1. You may give a piece to another player, if you see that it is needed.
2. You may not talk.
3. You may not gesture.
4. You may not take someone else's puzzle piece. You must wait to be given one.

Each group of five people is given an envelope with puzzle pieces. Each player within a group takes the pieces marked with a different letter of the alphabet. When everyone has a set of puzzle pieces, the process of creating five six-inch squares begins according to the ground rules stated above.

Once they have successfully accomplished the task, group members take a set of pieces marked with a different letter of the alphbet. The group starts the process again and tries to cooperate more effectively to reduce the amount of time that it takes for each person to make a six-inch square.

Inquiry

The facilitator guides the group sharing of information by adapting the questions and statements in the Activity Inquiry Fan to the content of this experience.

Samples:
What was the easiest part of this activity? What was the hardest?
How did the group demonstrate effective cooperation? How did that benefit the group?
How could the group improve the cooperative effort?

Five Squares—Six-Inch Puzzle

Directions for Making:

Cut tagboard or other substantial material according to the patterns given and mark each with the appropriate letter. All measurement is precise so that pieces interchange accurately. Place all of the A, B, C, D, and E pieces needed to complete the five six-inch puzzles in an envelope. Have the same number of envelopes as there are groups doing the activity.

Five Squares—Six-Inch Puzzle Patterns

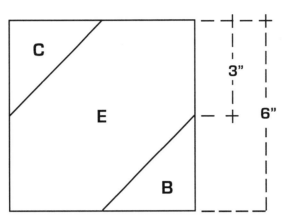

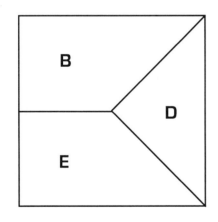

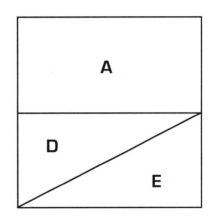

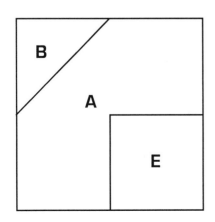

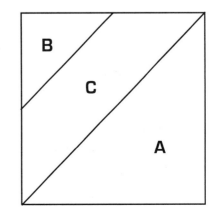

Think Tank
More Practice

Objective

Group members will practice the cooperative behaviors required of people to interact succcessfully with large numbers of people to complete a complex task.

Materials

Cardboard boxes and tubes, foil, packing pellets, different types of paper, tape, felt pens, scissors, glue, staplers, other available odds and ends

Procedure

The facilitator leads a discussion about how many adults today have the job of thinking up creative solutions to new problems. Then the group is challenged to become a "Think Tank" and create a prototype of a toy that:

- both girls and boys of all ages would like,
- is unlike any toy currently available,
- is small enough to fit in a shoe box,
- is nonviolent, and
- appeals to the imagination.

The group is given a table full of construction materials and proceeds to interact with one another to invent the toy described above. The facilitator intervenes only to refer group members to the list of cooperative behaviors, if it is necessary to keep the process moving. Once the prototype is completed, each member of the group explains a feature of the toy.

Inquiry

The facilitator guides the group sharing of information by adapting the questions and statements in the Activity Inquiry Fan to the content of this experience.

Samples:

Tell about how people used their imaginations to complete this cooperative project.

Talk about how "two heads are better than one."

How do you feel about the prototype the group designed?

Groups and Me
Transfer

Objective

Group members will reflect upon the benefits of cooperative endeavors and their feelings about cooperating in groups.

Materials

Journals, pens or pencils

Procedure

The facilitator asks group members to write in their journals about the following subjects sometime during the upcoming week:

Tell about what you like and don't like about working in groups.

Describe a time when you know that you really contributed something to a group. How did you feel?

Throughout the cooperation experiences, group members were encouraged to consider their own needs in relation to the needs of others. In *Chapter 10: Asserting Yourself*, group members explore behaviors that are developed to ensure that their individual perspective is clearly recognized within the group context and that their unique contributions are heard by others.

Facilitator Log

Things to remember:

_____
_____
_____
_____
_____
_____
_____
_____
_____
_____
_____
_____
_____
_____
_____
_____
_____
_____
_____
_____

Asserting
Yourself

Linda Lyon-Wright 1987

Chapter 10

Assertive skills are practiced as a part of People Skills training to reinforce feelings of self-worth and to enhance each group member's ability to make friends and successfully participate in cooperative activities. In addition, assertive behavior is a necessary feature of the more complex People Skills training ahead: Handling Verbal Abuse, Managing Strong Feelings, and Resolving Conflicts.

The assertiveness training presented here is basic and involves three levels. First, group members learn to identify passive, aggressive, and assertive behaviors on the basis of body language and the content of a statement. Next, participants practice making assertive statements, refusals, and requests. Finally, more complex interactions are explored, as participants learn assertive techniques for diffusing "power plays," thus avoiding power struggles with others.

Set I. Purpose:

To provide opportunities for group members to identify passive, aggressive, and assertive behaviors

Identifying Behaviors
Awareness

Objective

Group members will gain an awareness of what it means to be assertive by identifying the characteristics of passive, aggressive, and assertive behaviors.

Materials

"Passive, Aggressive, Assertive" cards (Experience 10.1) that are cut apart by the facilitator prior to the group meeting, puppets

Procedure

The facilitator explains the characteristics of passive, aggressive, and assertive behaviors. Puppets may be used with younger, less mature groups to act out passive, aggressive, and assertive behavior traits. Animal puppets are particularly effective tools (e.g., an alligator or lion for the "aggressive" character, a mouse or worm for the "passive" character, and a people puppet for the "assertive" character).

Passive: People who demonstrate passive behaviors:
1. often say "yes" when they want to say "no"
2. seem afraid to share real feelings or thoughts
3. have little or no eye contact with others
4. speak softly and infrequently
5. often slouch and shrug their shoulders

Aggressive: People who behave aggressively:
1. make statements without consideration for the feelings of others
2. often appear to be angry when really feeling hurt, embarrassed, sad, left out, frustrated, inadequate, or afraid
3. frequently abuse others physically and/or verbally
4. behave in a manner that is loud, threatening, insulting, and/or manipulative
5. are sometimes called a "bully"

Assertive: People who demonstrate assertive behaviors:
1. are honest and direct
2. choose to tell others what they like or dislike; want or don't want
3. speak in a calm, firm voice
4. look at others while speaking
5. accept responsibility for the choices they make

The facilitator models these behaviors or uses puppets for that purpose. For example, when discussing a passive person, the facilitator speaks in a quiet voice, slouches, shuffles feet, and/or uses other appropriate body language. Group members are asked to demonstrate these behaviors also. Next, the facilitator places the "Passive, Aggressive, Assertive" cards facedown in the center of the table and asks each group member in turn to choose a card, read it, and identify which type of behavior is defined by their card. Group members continue this process until all of the cards have been used.

Inquiry

The facilitator guides the group sharing of information by adapting the questions and statements in the Activity Inquiry Fan to the content of this experience.

Samples:
Think of two examples of aggressive behavior that you have experienced.
Name three people you consider to be assertive.
What are the possible benefits of assertive actions for yourself and others?

Passive, Aggressive, Assertive Behavior Cards

Directions: Copy this information onto cardstock and cut along the lines to form a deck of cards.
Shuffle the cards before using them.

Say "yes" when they mean "no"	Speak in a calm, firm voice
Are honest and direct	Frequently abuse others physically or verbally
Make statements without regard to the feelings of others	Speak softly and infrequently
Seem afraid to share real feelings or thoughts	Look at others while speaking
Choose to tell others what they like or dislike, want or don't want	Behave in a manner that is loud, threatening, insulting, and/or manipulative
Often appear to be angry when really feeling hurt, embarrassed, sad, left out, frustrated, inadequate, or afraid	Often slouch and shrug their shoulders
Have little or no eye contact with others	Accept responsibility for the choices they make

Which Is It: Passive, Aggressive, or Assertive?
Practice

Objective

Group members will gain practice being assertive by labeling statements and actions as being either passive, aggressive, or assertive.

Materials

Passive, Aggressive, Assertive sheet (Experiences 10.2 and 10.3), pencils

Procedure

Group members are given copies of either Experience 10.2 or 10.3. They are asked to complete the sheets with a partner or in triads to encourage discussion. When everyone has finished the exercise, personal insights gained in the small groups are shared with the entire group.

Inquiry

The facilitator guides the group sharing of information by adapting the questions and statements in the Activity Inquiry Fan to the content of this experience.

Samples:

What do you think someone "gets" by behaving either passively, assertively, and/or aggressively that would make them want to continue acting in this manner?

How does it feel to be in a situation that involves either passive, aggressive, or assertive behavior?

How could you teach this information to your friends?

Passive, Aggressive, or Assertive?

Level I

For the following situations, mark each response as:

AG = aggressive   AS = assertive   P = passive

Situation 1

Your teacher made a mistake correcting your spelling test.
Response:

_____ "Hey! You didn't do this right."

_____ Do nothing.

_____ "I think this word is spelled correctly. Would you check it again?"

Situation 2

You get the wrong change from a store clerk.
Response:

_____ Walk away and say nothing.

_____ "What are you trying to do—cheat me or something?"

_____ "Excuse me, I believe you gave me the wrong change."

Situation 3

Imagine a friend of yours asked to copy your homework.
Response:

_____ "No! That's cheating!"

_____ "I really spent a lot of time on this assignment. I don't want to let you copy my work."

_____ "I guess so."

Situation 4

You're playing a team game and some people on your team aren't participating.
Response:

_____ Say nothing.

_____ "If you're not going to play the game, get lost!"

_____ "I noticed you didn't participate with the team. Was something wrong?"

Situation 5

Someone asks you to go somewhere and you really don't want to go.
Response:

_____ "Are you kidding?"

_____ "Thanks for asking, and I'd rather not."

_____ "I don't think I can."

Situation 6

Your parents haven't talked to you about the notice you brought home from school about sign-ups for soccer. You really want to join the team.
Response:

_____ "Big help they are! They don't care if I have fun."

_____ Say nothing and hope someone brings it up.

_____ "I'd really like to play soccer. Here's information about signing up for the team."

Situation 7

You've just been offered some ice cream and you're allergic to milk.
Response:

_____ "No, thanks."

_____ "Well, I guess I could have a little."

_____ "You've got to be kidding! That stuff makes me sick!"

Passive, Aggressive, or Assertive?

Level II

For the following situations, mark each response as:

AG = aggressive   AS = assertive   P = passive

Situation 1

A teacher has made a mistake grading an exam.

Response:

_____ "You cheated me out of 10 points on this test!"

_____ Do nothing.

_____ "I've discovered an error in the way this exam was graded."

Situation 2

You get the wrong change from a store clerk.

Response:

_____ Walk away and say nothing.

_____ "What are you trying to do—cheat me or something?"

_____ "Excuse me, I believe you gave me the incorrect amount of money back."

Situation 3

Imagine a friend of yours asks to copy your homework.

Response:

_____ "No! That's cheating!"

_____ "I spent a lot of time on this assignment. I am unwilling to let you copy my work."

_____ "I guess so."

Situation 4

You're doing a group project and not all of the group members are doing their share of the work.

Response:

_____ Say nothing.

_____ "If you're not going to help with the project, just get out of here!"

_____ "I noticed that you haven't helped on our project. Is something wrong?"

Situation 5

Someone asks you to go somewhere and you really don't want to go.

Response:

_____ "Are you kidding?"

_____ "I appreciate the invitation, and I'd rather not."

_____ "I don't think I can."

Situation 6

You've been offered several jobs and want help deciding among them. No one has offered an opinion.

Response:

_____ "Big help they are! They don't care if I get the best job or not. They don't care about me."

_____ Say nothing and hope someone offers advice.

_____ "I've been giving this a lot of thought and need someone to help me. Are you willing to listen?"

Situation 7

You've just been offered alcohol at a party and you don't drink.

Response:

_____ "No, thank you."

_____ "Well, I guess I could have a little drink."

_____ "You've got to be kidding! Don't you know what that stuff does to your body!"

Journal Writing: Assertive Behaviors
Transfer

Objective

Group members will apply their knowledge of assertive behavior by watching for examples of it in daily living situations.

Materials

Journals, pens or pencils

Procedure

Group members are asked to pay close attention on a daily basis to their own and others' interactions. They are asked to record examples of assertive behavior and describe what made it seem assertive.

Set II. Purpose:

To provide opportunities for group members to (1) practice making assertive requests and refusals, and (2) practice giving constructive feedback

Analyzing Requests, Refusals, and Responses
Awareness

Objective

Group members will gain an awareness of the effectiveness of different ways of requesting, refusing, and responding.

Materials

Assertive Analysis (Experience 10.4)

Procedure

The facilitator asks volunteers from the group to read each example in Experience 10.4. After each one, members are asked to consider the following:

1. Does this tell you what the speaker really wants to say, or is the message hidden? What do you think the speaker is trying to say?
2. What might your response be if someone said this to you?
3. Is this an assertive statement? If not, change it into one.

Inquiry

The facilitator guides the group sharing of information by adapting the questions and statements in the Activity Inquiry Fan to the content of this experience.

Samples:

How does it feel to hear passive comments? How about aggressive comments?

Think about how you usually communicate with others. Are you usually assertive, aggressive, or passive? Talk about that.

What are three benefits that might arise from assertive communication?

Assertive Analysis

Requests

1. That cake really looks delicious. I bet it tastes good, too.

2. I need a piece of that cake. Give me a big one!

3. I'd really like a piece of cake. May I have some?

4. I don't suppose there's any extra cake?

5. If there's any cake left over, I'd like a piece.

6. Hi! I wonder if you'd consider sharing your cake with me?

Refusals

1. Don't be ridiculous! Of course, I don't want to run with you!

2. I don't think running is good for my knees.

3. I need new jogging shoes.

4. No, I don't want to run today.

5. No, I don't run, because running hurts my knees. I like to swim. We could do that together.

6. Gee, I'm not sure about that.

Responses

Statement: I don't think you are cut out for that job.

Response: I really don't care what you think!

Statement: I wonder if that job's for you.

Response: I've thought about it a lot. I'm going to try it for these reasons.

Statement: Have you really considered this job and all the work it involves?

Response: Gosh, I don't know about that.

Statement: Are you positive about taking this job?

Response: I feel there's some risk involved, and I'm prepared to accept that fact.

Saying "No"
Practice

Objective
Group members will become more effective communicators by mastering assertive refusal techniques.

Materials
"Role-play Situation Cards: Assertive Refusals" (Experiences 10.5 and 10.6)
Cards are cut apart by the facilitator prior to the group meeting.

Procedure
Group members are asked to offer the facilitator something (e.g. "Would you like to go to the movies?," "Would you like to come with my mom and me to the beach?," "Would you like something cold to drink?," etc.). The facilitator demonstrates an assertive refusal such as the following:

"No, thank you."
"No, I don't want to do that."
"No, I'd rather not."
"No, and thanks for asking."
"No, that's not something I want to do."
"No, I need to be alone now."
"No, I don't feel comfortable doing that."

Next, the facilitator leads a discussion and explains that all people have the right to choose what they do and do not want to do with their peers. The facilitator then asks group members to think of situations in which an assertive refusal would be appropriate, and also times when it would be inappropriate. The group is asked to consider possible consequences of using assertive refusals both (1) with parents or others in authority, and (2) when the request refutes a responsibility or an agreement previously made.

Members use the "Role-play Situation Cards," Level I or II, (Experience 10.5 or 10.6) to role play making assertive refusals.

Inquiry
The facilitator guides the group sharing of information by adapting the questions and statements in the Activity Inquiry Fan to the content of this experience.

Samples:
Think of a time in your past when you wish that you had said no. Describe the situation.
Pretend that you have a chance to relive the situation that you just described. Practice making a refusal.
Think of three of your best friends. Tell how you could teach them this information.

Role-Play Situation Cards:
Assertive Refusals
Level I

A classmate accuses you of cheating on a test. You know you didn't. You say:	A stranger offers you a ride home. You feel uncomfortable. You say:
Your friend wants you to join the soccer team. You aren't interested in joining. You say:	A neighbor who is going on vacation asks you to feed the pets. Your family already has something planned. You won't be able to do this. You say:
You are in a store and a friend asks you to help steal. You say:	A friend asks you to go bike riding. Your parents aren't home. You have to have their permission before you can go. You say:
Your best friend invites you to go to the movies. You are on restriction and know your parents won't let you go. You say:	A friend asks to copy your homework. You worked hard on yours. You say:
A friend asks you to play at recess. You don't want to play. You say:	A friend asks to look at some answers on your test. You say:

Role-Play Situation Cards:
Assertive Refusals
Level II

A friend accuses you of cheating on a test. You say:	Your best friend offers you a ticket to a great rock concert. You'd love to go. Your parents require chaperones. You say:
A friend asks to look at your answers on a test. You say:	A neighbor asks if you can baby-sit Friday night, but you already have plans. You say:
You are in a store. A friend asks you to steal something. You say:	Your older sister was on the high school basketball team. She wants you to sign up, and you're not interested. You say:
A friend offers you a ride in his dad's car. You know he doesn't have a driver's license. You say:	You are at a party and a friend offers you drugs. You say:
You are asked out by someone you don't want to date. You say:	A friend asks you to cut class together. You say:

Practicing Assertive Requests
More Practice

Objective

Group members become more effective communicators by practicing assertive requests.

Materials

"Role-play Situation Cards: Assertive Requests" (Experiences 10.7 and 10.8)
Cards are cut out by the facilitator prior to the group meeting.

Procedure

The facilitator writes the following four points about assertive requests on chart paper or the white board.

Assertive Requests
1. Look at the person
2. Be honest and direct
3. Speak in a calm, firm voice
4. Begin by using "I" statements, such as "I want ..." and "I need ..."

The facilitator tells group members that "making a request" means asking for something desired. In addition, the facilitator explains that "making assertive requests" is asking for something in a way that considers the feelings of others. When making an assertive request, one needs to consider the four points listed above.

The facilitator emphasizes that even though a person may ask for something assertively, the request may not always be granted. No one has control over how someone else will respond or act. However, certainly the chances of getting what one wants are less if a request is never made or an inappropriate request is made (whether passive or aggressive).

Before passing out the "Role-play Situation Cards," the facilitator models several role-play examples and uses an appropriate tone of voice and body language.

Inquiry

The facilitator guides the group sharing of information by adapting the questions and statements in the Activity Inquiry Fan to the content of this experience.

Samples:

Compare assertive refusals and assertive requests. Which is harder for you to do? Why?
Think of a time when you didn't ask for something that you really needed or wanted. How did you feel? How would you handle the situation differently now?

Role-Play Situation Cards:
Assertive Requests
Level I

You are buying something at a store. The salesclerk gives you the incorrect amount of change. You say: What might happen next?	You feel your parents should increase your allowance. You say: What might happen next?
You forget your homework assignment at your house. You need to tell your teacher. You say: What might happen next?	You are lost at an amusement park and go to a ticket booth for help. You say: What might happen next?
You see a group of kids playing together. You'd like to join them. You say: What might happen next?	You don't understand how to do some math problems. You want your teacher to explain it again. You say: What might happen next?
Several of your friends are going to a movie together. They haven't invited you and you want to join them. You say: What might happen next?	You asked your mom a week ago if you could go to summer camp. She hasn't given you an answer and you'd like to know. You say: What might happen next?
A friend borrowed one of your toys and hasn't returned it. You'd like it back. You say: What might happen next?	A friend borrowed some money from you and hasn't returned it. You need it to buy something. You say: What might happen next?

Role-Play Situation Cards:
Assertive Requests
Level II

You buy a new pair of pants and discover they are ripped when you get them home. You take them back to the salesclerk. You say: What might happen next?	You are taking a math class and don't understand a new concept. You would like your teacher to explain it again. You say: What might happen next?
You want to join a group of friends who are playing ball. You say: What might happen next?	You are in a department store and need to find a restroom. You say: What might happen next?
A friend has been teasing you about your new haircut. You say: What might happen next?	You audition for a play and want to participate. The director turns you down. You say: What might happen next?
You are with several friends who are going to a movie. They haven't invited you, and you want to join them. You say: What might happen next?	A friend borrowed $10 from you and hasn't returned it. You say: What might happen next?
You are standing in line to buy tickets, and someone cuts in front of you. You say: What might happen next?	You are at a restaurant and haven't been waited on yet. After fifteen minutes you decide to go talk to the head waiter. You say: What might happen next?

Journal Writing: "Please" and "No, Thank You"
Transfer

Objective

Group members will write about assertive requests and refusals that they make in their daily lives.

Materials

Journals, pens or pencils

Procedure

Group members are asked to write in their journals one time during the week when they made an assertive request and one time when they made an assertive refusal. They also are asked to note any strong examples of assertive requests and refusals made by members of their family or by their friends.

Set III. Purpose:

To provide opportunities for group members to practice assertive techniques to diffuse "power plays" and pave the way for cooperative problem solving

Power Plays
Awareness

Objective

Group members will gain an awareness of the features of a "power play" in order to know when to apply an assertive tool to improve the outcome of the situation.

Materials

"Power Plays" sheets (Experiences 10.9 and 10.10)

Procedure

The facilitator leads group members through a discussion of the occurrence of power plays in daily living. Information about "power plays" includes the following:
- They are human interactions in which someone "wins" and someone "loses."
- Strong emotions usually accompany power plays.
- Learning to diffuse "power plays" in an assertive manner always considers the needs and desires of all people involved. It is a step toward becoming a "peacemaker," someone who peacefully resolves conflicts with others.

Next, group members read through the power play samples in Experience 10.9 or 10.10, noting the win/lose qualities of each. They also identify the feelings that probably accompany the scenarios.

Inquiry

The facilitator guides the group sharing of information by adapting the questions and statements in the Activity Inquiry Fan to the content of this experience.

Samples:
Tell about a "power play" you've experienced in your own life.
Describe how you would handle that situation differently now.
Pretend you're teaching someone about being a "peacemaker." What would you say?

Power Plays

Level I

Scene I

Person #1: Let's play ball this afternoon.

Person #2: I told Jeff I'd go rollerblading.

Person #1: Fine! Go ahead and do what he says all the time. I hate rollerblading.

Person #2: We went rollerblading last week. I thought you had fun. Come join us!

Person #1: I bet you weren't even going to ask me! Listen, forget about rollerblading today or forget our friendship!

Scene II

Person #1: Jessie, you need a new pair of shoes. Those don't match your clothes.

Person #2: Gosh, I kind of like them.

Person #1: Look, they go better with my jeans than with yours. Tell you what— I'll give you my shoes and take those off your hands.

Person #2: My shoes are pretty new.

Person #1: Are you saying mine aren't? Hey, if you think I'm trying to cheat you, just say so! I was just trying to help you out!

Person #2: Gee, thanks for helping me. I guess I don't match things too well, but I kind of like my new shoes.

Apply these four points to each scene:
1. Who was winner/loser in each scene?
2. How do you think each person was feeling?
3. How could being assertive have helped end these "power plays?"
4. "Replay" each scene and and change what person #2 says into an assertive response.

Power Plays
Level II

Scene I

Person #1: I need to talk with you. You need to get straight about my conversation with Jan.

Person #2: I don't need to "get straight" about anything! But I'll tell you a thing or two.

Person #1: What on earth could you, who "knows-it-all," tell me?

Person #2: I could tell you that you are constantly poking around in my business!

Person #1: (in tears) If you must know, it's just because I care about you!

Scene II

Person #1: I made reservations for a ski weekend for us!

Person #2: Gosh, I'm not sure I want to do that.

Person #1: You'll love it! You can take lessons while I head for the mountaintops!

Person #2: Gee, I don't have warm enough clothes or boots or anything.

Person #1: The trouble with you is you're so afraid to try new things. You absolutely need this adventure!

Person #2: I guess I could try it out. I'd prefer a quiet weekend at home.

Person #1: Good heavens! How dull! Lighten up already!

Person #2: (halfheartedly) You're probably right. When are we going?

Consider these questions for each scene:
1. Who was winner/loser in each scene?
2. How do you think each person was feeling?
3. How could being assertive have helped end these "power plays?"
4. Replay each scene and and change what person #2 says into an assertive response.

Assertive Techniques
More Awareness

Objective

Group members will identify and practice the assertive techniques of (1) broken record, (2) inquiry, and (3) paraphrasing to effectively diffuse "power plays."

Materials

Assertive Skills (Experience 10.11) and Power Plays (Experiences 10.9 and 10.10)

Procedure

Group members join in a discussion of the three assertive techniques that are defined on the accompanying exercise sheet (Experience 10.11). They are then asked to apply the techniques to the two "power plays" presented in the previous awareness exercise. The facilitator asks for volunteers to role-play the people in the scenes and use one of the three assertive techniques to diffuse the "power plays."

Inquiry

The facilitator guides the group sharing of information by adapting the questions and statements in the Activity Inquiry Fan to the content of this experience.

Samples:

With whom do you think you'll feel comfortable using these new skills?

Think of a situation from the past. How could you handle it differently now that you have this information?

How could a friend of yours take the information we have learned in this activity and use it at home, at school, and with friends?

Three Assertive Techniques:
Broken Record, Inquiry, Paraphrasing

Broken Record is demonstrated by repeating what another person has said and consistently asserting your position. This technique is not effective in emotionally volatile situations in which people are very angry or hostile.

Example:

#1: "I want to go to the arcade tonight."

#2: "I understand that you want to go to the arcade tonight, and I don't have any way to get you there."

#1: "But everyone is going tonight. I have to go."

#2: "I understand that you want to go to the arcade with everyone tonight, and I don't have any way to get you there."

#1: "Why can't you buy a new car? It's not fair!"

#2: "I understand that you think it's unfair to miss going to the arcade, and I have no way of getting you there."

Inquiry is demonstrated by actively encouraging criticism to gain information. Inquiring tends to calm the other person by showing that you are really listening to their perspective without allowing them to blame you for their upset.

Example:

#1: You really bugged me when you went hiking with Charlie.

#2: Really? What exactly was it that bothered you?

#1: You didn't ask me to go along.

#2: I don't quite understand. Tell me more, will you?

#1: You don't seem to want to do things with me anymore.

#2: How do you feel about that?

#1: Upset, left out, hurt.

#2: What would help?

Paraphrasing occurs when someone's message restated by you demonstrates that the person was heard.

Example:

#1: I was wondering why you volunteered to organize the class picnic. You know I did that last year and really had fun. Everyone says I do a great job. No one else ever wants to do it. Now you go and say you'll do it. I'm left out.

#2: You're wondering why I volunteered for a position you've done such a good job with before. I understand that you feel badly about my organizing this year's picnic.

Role-Playing Assertive Techniques
Practice

Objective

Group members will gain more communication skill by applying the three assertive techniques (broken record, inquiry, and paraphrasing) to real-life situations.

Materials

"Assertive Role-Play Dialogues" (Experience10.12), white board or chart paper, blank drawing paper, markers

Procedure

The facilitator asks group members to read the role-play dialogues presented in Experience10.12. Pairs volunteer to act out each scene as written and then attempt to utilize assertive techniques to alter the scenario and diffuse the "power play."

Next, group members are asked to describe or draw a picture to illustrate a real-life "power play" each has experienced. On chart paper or a white board, the facilitator writes out the dialogue from the situations that group members express. A pair of group members act out the scene and attempt to redirect what happened by using one of the three assertive techniques practiced: broken record, inquiry, or paraphrasing.

Inquiry

The facilitator guides the group sharing of information by adapting the questions and statements in the Activity Inquiry Fan to the content of this experience.

Samples:

How do you think these assertive tools will benefit you in your daily life?

Create an activity that you could use to teach your friends this information.

Tell about "power plays" in your own words.

Assertive Role-Play Dialogues

Scene I

#1: Go get my books for me.

#2: Get your own books. You sure are lazy.

#1: Knock off the name-calling! I happen to be really tired. A real friend would just go get the books!

#2: Looks like I'm just not a real friend then! (stomps off)

Scene II

#1: If you want me to do my homework, then buy me that album I want.

#2: Okay, Honey. I'll get it for you tomorrow.

#1: No way! Go out and get it now, and then I'll hit the books.

#2: Now, Honey, please be reasonable. The stores are closed.

Scene III

#1: We're going to lose this game if you don't get to practice every day.

#2: Everyone wants me to be perfect!

#1: This game is bigger than any other game. You get to practice!

#2: Take a hike!

#1: I can complain to the coach, and don't think I won't!

Scene IV

#1: I want you home after school. No job!

#2: I'll do as I please!

#1: Your grades are going to fall if you work.

#2: Nonsense!

#1: No job!

#2: Want to bet?

Journal Writing: Nurture a Friendship
Transfer

Objective

Group members will apply assertive techniques to improve one significant relationship in their daily lives.

Materials

Journals, pens or pencils

Procedure

The facilitator asks group members to choose one important relationship that could be improved by using one of the three assertive techniques that they have learned: broken record, inquiry, or paraphrasing. During the week ahead they are asked to try using a selected assertive tool when they have difficulty with the relationship that they chose. The facilitator offers assistance to help group members decide which technique would be the most appropriate to use: broken record if someone is particularly stubborn or "pushy," inquiry if someone is very sensitive and gets hurt easily, and paraphrasing if someone is a "thinking" kind of person who needs to know that who they are and what they think are important.

The cooperative skills and assertive techniques fostered in the previous sections prepare group members for the more complex interactions that are the topics of the final three chapters of the Belonging Program. *Handling Verbal Abuse, Managing Strong Feelings,* and *Resolving Conflicts* require group members to draw upon the entire storehouse of skills and inner resources developed thus far in People Skills training.

Facilitator Log

Things to remember:

_____

_____

_____

_____

_____

_____

_____

_____

_____

_____

_____

_____

_____

_____

_____

_____

_____

_____

_____

_____

_____

Handling
Verbal Abuse

Linda Lyon-Wright 1987

Chapter 11

The themes of the final three chapters of *Belonging* require group members to integrate the skills that they have learned thus far and apply them in complex situations. The activities in this chapter challenge group members to deal with verbal abuse that they have expressed or have received from others. The visual image of thorns on a rose bush is used to remind group members that verbal abuse pierces through a person's protective shield and gives rise to painful emotional reactions. In addition, it is pointed out that abusive verbal exchanges frequently escalate into violent physical confrontations. Because of the increasing number of children who are victims of violence and who have turned to violent actions as a means of solving problems, it is crucial that young people acquire effective tools to diffuse potentially volatile situations at a verbal level.

The activities presented here are designed to help group members deal with verbal abuse from both a victim and an offender perspective. Group members examine their life experiences with verbal abuse and the feelings they hold related to these events. They explore how to shield or protect themselves from cruel remarks and how to effectively respond to them. The group considers why people resort to verbal abuse, i.e., what is the person really trying to say or make happen? Those who have engaged in verbal abuse gain insight into their actions in a nonjudgmental environment, are given an opportunity to choose new behaviors, and are supported in their attempts to change the way that they treat others.

Set I. Purpose:

To provide opportunities for group members to disclose life experiences with verbal abuse, examine the connection between verbal and physical abuse, and practice effective responses

Words Do Hurt
Awareness

Objective

Group members will explore verbal and physical abuse in terms of the thoughts and feelings associated with the abusive behaviors.

Materials

Chart paper, marking pens

Procedure

The facilitator labels and posts the chart paper in the same manner as the sample below. Group members are asked to brainstorm examples of verbal abuse that they—or people they know—have experienced. Examples to stimulate discussion include actions such as swearing, name-calling, humiliation, intimidation, provoking, lying, and spreading rumors. These are recorded on the chart under the "verbal" category. Next to each example of verbal abuse on the chart, group members give examples of any physical abuse that might accompany the verbal abuse (e.g., a shove while name-calling, getting right up in someone's face when trying to intimidate, etc.). Members list feelings, both of the victim and the offender, in the final column.

Perceptions of Abuse		
Verbal	*Physical*	*Feelings of the Victim and the Offender*

Inquiry

The facilitator guides the group sharing of information by adapting the questions and statements in the Activity Inquiry Fan to the content of this experience.

Samples:

What might the person be thinking before saying each of the examples of verbal abuse listed above? For example, someone who says "You fool!" could be thinking, "I feel jealous because you had a better idea than I did."

What do you think makes people respond in different ways to the same abusive comment. Why do some people get mad, some get hurt, and others feel very frightened?

How do you typically respond when someone says something abusive to you?

Five-Step Assertive Response Model
Practice

Objective
Group members will gain skill handling verbal abuse by practicing assertive responses.

Materials
Model of the Five-Step Assertive Response (presented below), "Role-Play Situations" (Experience 11.1), Support Group Update (Form 11.2)

Procedure
The facilitator writes the following *Five-Step Assertive Response Model* on chart paper or on the white board for display. This is the same model that was used to practice effective responses in *Chapter 10: Asserting Yourself*. In addition to the Five-Step Model, the group is introduced to *Splash of Cold Water* words, which represent a simple—yet very effective—tool for handling verbal abuse in a manner that doesn't cause the situation to escalate. When someone makes a derogatory comment, the splash-of-cold-water response is something like, "You may be right about that." or "I never considered that about myself. I'll really think about that." The response is meant to surprise the other person, which changes the tone of what is transpiring, even to the point of stopping the verbal abuse before it goes any further.

Group members are again cautioned to use these response tools with their peers and with only those adults who know and use these same assertive tools. To increase the arena within which group members can use assertive tools, it is helpful for facilitators to inform and/or train other willing adults who are active in the lives of the group members. The letter provided as Form 11.2 can be sent to parents or guardians of group members and shared with teachers, therapists, and other significant adults to inform them of the assertive language that group members are learning and to enlist their cooperation.

Five-Step Assertive Response Model
1. Cool off and ask to speak with the other person.
2. "I don't like it when _____."
3. "I feel _____ when _____."
4. "Instead of _____, I'd appreciate _____."
5. "I think this will benefit us both because _____."

Next, group members are asked to act out possible responses to the role-play situations in Experience 11.1 by using the Five-Step Assertive Response Model or Splash of Cold Water words.

Inquiry
The facilitator guides the group sharing of information by adapting the questions and statements in the Activity Inquiry Fan to the content of this experience.

Samples:
How did it feel to assert yourself in these situations?
Name three people with whom you could use the Five-Step Model and/or Splash of Cold Water words?
When would you choose not to use these approaches?

Role-Play Situations:
Handling Verbal Abuse

1. A friend calls you a "chicken" to provoke a fight.

2. Your partner in P.E. says that you're an uncoordinated moron.

3. An old friend of yours says "I'm leaving" as soon as you sit down.

4. Your best friend laughs at your new haircut.

5. Your brother swears at you.

6. A group member teases you because you just got braces.

7. Your athletic sister laughs at you when you don't make the baseball team.

8. Your cousin teases you when your report card isn't as good as hers.

9. A friend starts a rumor about you and a boy in your class.

10. Your brother rolls his eyes when he's told you have to sit next to each other in the car.

Support Group Update

We have been practicing many People Skills—things you need to know to get along with yourself and others—over the past weeks. Right now we're working on a particularly difficult task, learning to respond assertively to words and actions rather than engaging in argument or pretending nothing is wrong. We are learning a Five-Step Assertive Response Model that looks and sounds like this:

1. Cool off and ask the person if you can talk to them.

2. Say: "I don't like it when _____."

3. Say: "I feel _____ when _____."

4. Say: "Instead of _____, I'd appreciate_____."

5. Say: "I think this would benefit us both because _____."

You can help by talking about the model, using it yourself, or listening to _____ practice it in your day-to-day interactions.
(group member's name)

Thank You.

Journal Writing: Behind Verbal Abuse
Transfer

Objective

Group members will apply their knowledge of what motivates people to engage in verbal abuse and ways to handle such abuse to their daily lives.

Materials

Journals, pens and pencils

Procedure

The facilitator asks group members to write down examples of verbal abuse that is directed toward them or others during the upcoming week. They are asked to guess the intention of the person engaging in the verbal abuse: What is that person really trying to say? Group members also write down how they or someone else responded to the comments or actions.

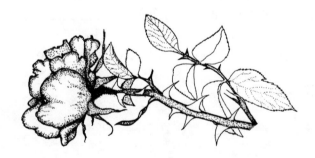

Set II. Purpose:
To help group members learn ways of reducing internal tension without abusing others

Tension Reducers
Awareness

Objective
Group members will identify Tension Reducer activities that one could perform in lieu of saying or doing something abusive to someone.

Materials
Chart paper or white board, markers

Procedure
The facilitator charts out the following information:

Feeling	Abusive Reactions	Tension Reducer
Anger	Swear Intimidate—"You better watch out." Call names	
Jealousy	Humiliate—"I can't believe you didn't know that!" Start rumors	
Sad or Hurt	Abandon—"I'm not your friend anymore." Retaliate/Hurt back	
Fear	All of the above to mask the fear	

Group members are asked to brainstorm other Abusive Reactions they or people they know demonstrate and to place these in relation to one of the feelings on the chart. Next, they list Tension Reducer activities that they or someone else could do instead of engaging in these habitual Abusive Reactions. Tension Reducer activities are defined as actions that could be taken in the moment to make someone stop before doing something to hurt another person. Examples of such activities are: (1) take a deep breath, (2) count to 10 in your head, (3) walk away and continue walking for a while, (4) identify a code word or image as a reminder not to react abusively, and/or (5) squeeze or rub your hands together. The group then discusses the probable effectiveness of each idea.

Inquiry
The facilitator guides the group sharing of information by adapting the questions and statements in the Activity Inquiry Fan to the content of this experience.

Samples:
Name three Tension Reducers that would help you or someone you know.
Which types of Verbal Abuse have you experienced in your life? Were you the victim or the offender?
Apply this information to the world around you. Which feeling states do you think lead to the most problems?

Time-out/Look Inside
Practice

Objective

Group members will practice two introspective Tension Reducer exercises to help them refrain from engaging in verbal abuse in the future.

Materials

Contemplative, instrumental music tape; colored pens (a set of different colors for each group member), "Look Inside!" Mandala (Experience 11.3)

Procedure

Part 1: Focused Time-out: The facilitator asks group members to choose a comfortable, private place in the room and sit or lie there. They are then guided to assume the body posture of someone who is upset: angry, sad, jealous, hurt, or scared. Next, they are instructed to silently say "I feel (feeling word)" and picture in their mind a situation in which they actually felt this way until they are able to remember the sensations of that emotion. When everyone has accomplished this in some way, the facilitator instructs group members to breathe deeply—in through the nose, out through the mouth. They are told to continue this steady breathing pattern until asked to stop in five minutes. Music may be added to the background. At the end of the five-minute breathing time, group members are asked to return to a circle and share how this Focused Time-out affected their feeling state. They are also asked to share anything that they thought or imagined while breathing and "tuning in" to themselves.

Part 2: Mandala: Group members are asked to repeat Part 1: Focused Time-out using a different emotion. This time, after two or three minutes of continuous breathing, the facilitator asks each to imagine an object or symbol that could represent a calm, peaceful feeling for them. This could be anything (eg., an object in nature, a design, a symbol, a person, etc.). When everyone has something in mind, the Look Inside! Mandala (Experience 11.3) and packs of colored pens are distributed. Group members are asked to draw their special object in the middle circle. The facilitator explains that a mandala, which means "circle" in Sanskrit, is a circular drawing in which all designs radiate from a center much like petals on a flower or the iris of the human eye. Group members are guided to draw whatever shapes, lines, figures, or other forms they like in the blank spaces that grow from the central circle on the mandala. They are reminded that the center symbol represents them at peace, so the forms and colors used to surround it could reflect that feeling state, as well. Reflective music can be played to add to the quiet, focused, introspective nature of the drawing.

These mandalas are examined in a follow-up group discussion. The facilitator points out how these types of introspective experiences allow people to work through their own inner conflict to effectively "interact" with others, rather than "react" in old, habitual ways.

Inquiry

The facilitator guides the group sharing of information by adapting the questions and statements in the Activity Inquiry Fan to the content of this experience.

Samples:

Pretend that you are teaching a group of friends about Focused Time-outs and Mandalas. What would your directions be?

How did your feelings change during different parts of this experience? Which feeling did you have at the beginning, middle, and end?

Tell about the significance of the central symbol in your mandala.

Look Inside!

Color Combination
Transfer

Objective

Group members will apply their knowledge of the importance of Tension Reducers to complete an art expression/journal writing activity.

Materials

Journals, colored pens

Procedure

Group members are instructed to choose a colored marker to represent an upset feeling that they frequently experience. Next, each is asked to select a marker to stand for a peaceful, calm feeling—a color that really makes that person feel good. The facilitator asks group members to use these colors in their journals sometime during the upcoming week in the following manner:

"On a journal page that is on the left side of the open book, make a scribble using the "upset" color.

On the page to the right side of this, create a doodle in the "calm, peaceful" color.

Finally, draw for a third time using both colors, with the peaceful color completely surrounding the upset color.

Last of all, write as if you were the upset color and tell (1) why you are upset and (2) how the peaceful color can help.

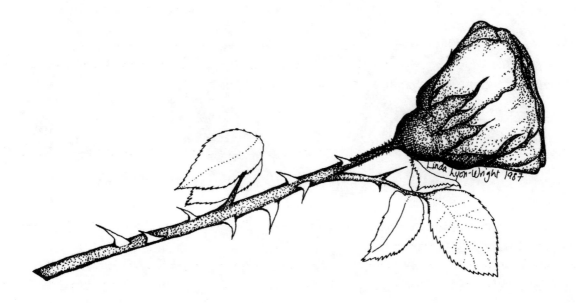

Set III. Purpose:

To help group members learn ways to protect themselves from the potential pain of verbal abuse and to lessen the effect it has on them

This Is Who I Am
Awareness

Objective

Group members will become aware of the protective power of a strong sense of personal worth.

Materials

Reflective, instrumental music; drawing paper, paints, felt pens, colored chalk or pastels

Procedure

The facilitator leads a discussion about the importance of growing strong in the knowledge of one's personal worth. Group members are guided toward the realization that one solid protection against verbal abuse is to have a secure knowledge of their own inherent value. They are asked to consider that all people are worthwhile and valuable simply because they exist. The more clearly people get in touch with this, the less likely the actions of others will shake their equilibrium and cause serious upset.

Next, group members are asked to sit quietly with their bodies loose and relaxed. When all are comfortable, they are asked to close or cover their eyes and turn their attention inward. The facilitator reads the following passage:

"Take a walk in your imagination, down a path of smooth stone, beneath an archway of green trees. A cool breeze brushes against your face and carries the fragrance of wildflowers. The soft noises of forest creatures and the water sounds of a nearby stream add to the perfect calm of your walk. You move easily and happily toward a clearing right in the center of this place in your imagination. You notice how everything looks, smells, and sounds. You pick a piece of sweet grass and taste it. Standing right here in the center of the clearing, you are sure of your place in nature and you are certain that you are as valuable as anything that you are appreciating—just because you are here."

The facilitator allows for a few moments of silence. Group members then are asked to open their eyes and paint, draw, or write about the peaceful, centered, unshakeable place they imagined. These images and the guided imagery experience are shared in a follow-up discussion.

Inquiry

The facilitator guides the group sharing of information by adapting the questions and statements in the Activity Inquiry Fan to the content of this experience.

Samples:

Compare this approach to handling verbal abuse with the Five-Step Assertive Response Model. How are they the same? How are they different?

Name three possible ways that knowing you are worthwhile protects you from verbal abuse?

Make up a guided experience that you could use to bring yourself or someone else to a calm place in the imagination.

Letters from Me to Me
Practice

Objective

Group members will experience the protective power of a strong sense of self worth in relationship to verbal abuse.

Materials

Writing and drawing paper, pens, pencils, markers, paper shredder or scissors

Procedure

Group members are asked to consider a past problem that they have had with either giving or receiving verbal abuse. They are asked to draw a picture of the situation, which could be a realistic depiction or an abstract representation of how they felt. The facilitator makes it clear that the pictures and letters that the group will produce in this session will not leave the room.

Next, they write a letter to the other person or people involved and express what they thought and felt during and after the incident. Group members are encouraged to be very direct and thorough even to the point of exagerating (e.g., "What you said to me stands out as one of the most devastating experiences of my life. I thought you were a horrible person to say such cruel things. I feel sorry for you, if you get some sort of sick pleasure from hurting others."). If they are writing about verbal abuse that they gave, group members are encouraged to compose thoughtful apologies to those who were offended (e.g., "I am so sorry for the rumors that I started about you. I know that they caused you a lot of embarassment. I wish that I could take it back, but I can't. I know that I won't choose to do that ever again.").

The facilitator asks if anyone would like to share with the group, after which group members use a paper shredder or scissors to destroy the pictures and letters. A follow-up discussion is held to examine the value of writing letters that are not meant to be sent, but rather to release the thoughts and feelings related to an unpleasant circumstance.

Variation:

Sometimes people decide that directly approaching an offending person would not be safe or useful. In addition to writing letters that are never sent, some people benefit from venting their feelings out loud. The facilitator points out to group members the value of asking a trusted friend to just listen as they express (even yell) their thoughts, feelings, and wishes. The friend may be asked not to give advice, but rather to be supportive by just listening.

Inquiry

The facilitator guides the group sharing of information by adapting the questions and statements in the Activity Inquiry Fan to the content of this experience.

Samples:

Compare this method of handling verbal abuse with the Five-Step Assertive Response Model. How are they the same? How are they different? When would you use this approach?

How does an activity such as this protect someone from the hurtful effects of verbal abuse?

How did it feel to draw the picture? write the letter? shred the letter?

Journal Writing: Choose Again
Transfer

Objective
Group members will apply their knowledge of handling verbal abuse to real-life situations.

Materials
Journals, pens and pencils

Procedure
The facilitator asks group members to consider how hard it can be to change old habits. Sometimes people feel so guilty about making poor choices that they aren't able to really admit past mistakes and become free to choose new ways of being. Sometimes others won't allow someone to change even when the person is making incredible efforts to demonstrate improved behavior. Group members are asked to write or draw in their journals about a behavior change they would like to make and three ways trusted people in their lives could help them make the change. After reflecting in their journals, they are asked to share the information they wrote with one friend or family member to enlist their support.

The information and People Skills explored in this section allowed group members to understand the feelings and actions of both the victim and the offender in verbally abusive exchanges. They practiced a variety of methods for handling verbal abuse directed toward them and techniques to keep themselves from verbally abusing others. They learned how to protect themselves from the emotional effects of abusive encounters and to be bold enough to choose different strategies when confronted with the fact that their actions hurt others. In *Chapter 12: Managing Strong Feelings*, group members develop a deeper understanding of human emotions and what they have to tell by examining some of life's harder lessons.

Facilitator Log

Things to remember:

_____

_____

_____

_____

_____

_____

_____

_____

_____

_____

_____

_____

_____

_____

_____

_____

_____

_____

_____

_____

_____

*Managing
Strong Feelings*

Chapter 12

"Anger Management" is currently one of the most popular support group themes for children and adolescents. Although all of the People Skills in the Belonging Program build upon each other, the material in this chapter could stand alone as the content of a group focused on managing anger. Since anger frequently is a mask for fear or sorrow, it is appropriate to consider these three strong feelings together.

Learning about intense and complex feelings, their unique qualities and functions, makes sense in light of the fact that human emotions accompany all significant experiences in life. As group members continue to approach emotions as "energy in motion," they learn that paying attention and moving through strong feelings allows them to protect themselves from dangerous situations, heal from traumatic events, and make changes when something is wrong.

The importance of having a Circle of Support to help individuals deal with life stresses and the strong feelings of fear, anger, and sorrow that come with them, is also addressed in the upcoming activities. In addition, group members gain further practice using the Five-Step Assertive Response Model from the previous chapter as they expand their ability to know when, where, and with whom to apply this approach when managing strong feelings. All of this work further prepares the group for its final frontier in *Chapter 13: Resolving Conflicts.*

Set I. Purpose:

To provide opportunities for group members to recognize the physical sensations and behavioral indicators of strong feelings

Body Full of Feeling
Awareness

Objective

Group members will gain an awareness of the physical features of the "big three" strong emotions by brainstorming descriptors of fear, sorrow, and anger and their relationship to specific life events.

Materials

Chart paper, felt pens

Procedure

The facilitator lists the following headings on separate sheets of chart paper:

• Fear: signals danger and seeks to protect us
• Sorrow: signals a change and seeks to soothe our loss
• Anger: signals that something is wrong and seeks to push us to act

Underneath these titles, a line is drawn down the middle of each chart. The left column is used for listing life events which elicit each of the feelings. The right column is used to describe the physical sensations and behaviors a person might demonstrate when experiencing each feeling under each of the different circumstances. Examples of how the charts will look are presented on page 223.

Recorders are selected for each of the listed feelings. Group members are directed to brainstorm for all categories at once. Such a "buzz" of ideas sometimes breaks down inhibitions and encourages honesty.

Inquiry

The facilitator guides the group sharing of information by adapting the questions and statements in the Activity Inquiry Fan to the content of this experience.

Samples:
Which of these strong feelings is most familiar to you?
At this point in your life, what do you do to manage your strong feelings?
Name three examples of life events that you heard about today and the feelings associated with them.

Fear: Signals danger and seeks to protect us

Life Events	Physical Sensations and Behaviors
Ex.: Someone followed me home.	Heart pounded. Walked faster.

Sorrow: Signals change and seeks to soothe our losses

Life Events	Physical Sensations and Behaviors
Ex.: Boyfriend broke up with me.	Felt weak. Cried.

Anger: Signals that something is wrong and seeks to push us to act

Life Events	Physical Sensations and Behaviors
Ex.: Someone started a rumor about my family.	Felt hot. Muscles tensed.

Strong Feelings Scripts
Practice

Objective

Group members will gain practice labeling strong feelings after identifying behaviors that demonstrate those feelings.

Materials

"Strong Feelings" scripts (Experiences 12.1 and 12.2)

Procedure

Group members are asked to volunteer to read the "Strong Feelings" scripts. The first reading is uninterrupted. During the second reading, the facilitator stops the action periodically to ask how the group thinks a character is feeling and how they came to this decision (e.g., what behaviors told them a character was feeling a certain way.).

Inquiry

The facilitator guides the group sharing of information by adapting the questions and statements in the Activity Inquiry Fan to the content of this experience.

Samples:

What were the different emotions expressed by the family members? How did each show the feeling?
What do you think will happen next?
Which family member(s) reacted the way that you might? Talk about that.

Strong Feelings Script
Level I

Identify strong feelings and how different people demonstrate them.

Narrator: The scene is the home of Mr. King, who is a single parent raising his three sons—Matt, Jonathan, and Chris. Mr. King's girlfriend is coming for dinner. He is rushing, trying to get prepared, and is behind schedule.

Mr. King: OK guys! Stop watching TV right now! I told you to help and I mean it!

Matt: Oh brother, more work! (He turns the TV up louder and ignores his dad.)

Mr. King: Turn that off! Two of you do the dishes and one of you vacuum.

Chris: I get to vacuum.

Matt: No, I do. You always get to do it. (pushes Chris)

Chris: You creep! (shoves Matt, who falls over a chair)

Jonathan: He's bleeding! He's bleeding! He's really hurt! (starts to cry)

Chris: I'm really sorry, Matt. (His face is white.)

Mr. King: (walks in, sees the mess, and clenches his fists) What happened?

Jonathan: Boy, are we going to get it! (runs and locks himself in the bathroom)

Chris: I'm sorry, Dad. (puts his hand on Matt's shoulder and lowers his head)

Matt: Do I need stitches, Dad? (hands shaking)

Mr. King: We better go have someone check it out. (doorbell rings)

Narrator: Mr. King's girlfriend walks in, opens her mouth, and freezes at the sight before her.

Strong Feelings Script
Level II

Identify the strong feelings and how different people demonstrate them.

Narrator: Ms. James is driving home from work with news that will affect her family. Her boss has asked her to travel to several conventions, which will take her away from her family for days at a time. She imagined the reactions of her husband Kyle and her daughters, Gina and Camilla.

Ms. James: (at the dinner table) I have some news for everyone. (Her voice is low and she clears her throat.) I have been asked to attend a series of conventions this year. That will mean traveling two to three days some weeks. (She searches their faces.)

Camilla: That will mean more baby sitters. I hate baby sitters, and I hate you! (cries)

Mr. James: (voice quiet, and picking at his food) I think it sounds exciting.

Camilla: Exciting? It's lousy news! (throws her spoon down and races out of the room)

Gina: (wringing her napkin) Who's going to take me to dance lessons and soccer practice on those days? Do I have to give that up?

Ms. James: No, of course not. We'll work that all out, or I won't accept the position. (pleading voice) Come on, I need everyone's cooperation.

Mr. James: (sits back and sighs) This is going to be hard on me.

Ms. James: (covers her face and nods her head up and down)

Gina: Cheer up, Mom. (pats her arm)

Feelings in Pictures
Transfer

Objective

Group members will apply their knowledge of strong feelings and the expression of those feelings independently.

Materials

Magazine pictures of people demonstrating a variety of strong feelings, journals, pens and pencils

Procedure

At the end of a group meeting, the facilitator gives each group member a "people picture" cut from a magazine. They are asked to glue the picture in their journal and write a statement in their journals about how the person is feeling, how they came to that conclusion, and what they think happened to bring about the particular feeling state.

Set II. Purpose:

To provide opportunities for group members to address ways of handling the "Big Three" Strong Feelings: Fear, Sorrow and Anger

Bottling Fear
Awareness

Objective

Group members will gain awareness of the relationship between effectively managing fear and their overall well-being as a person.

Materials

Clear glass bottle or jar with a lid, slips of blank paper, pens or pencils, butcher paper, colored markers, crayons, or chalk

Procedure

The facilitator leads a discussion about the function of fear: to warn us of danger, either real or perceived. Group members are given information about how living in a constant state of fear inhibits a person's ability to experience a full range of emotions, enjoy the richness of daily living, and/or learn new things. People who do not learn healthy ways to manage fear may become numbed or paralyzed by their fear. Other people who live in fear seem to be constantly on the run to avoid confronting it.

After a discussion of the above ideas, the facilitator places a stack of blank slips of paper and pencils in the middle of the table along with an empty clear glass bottle or jar. Group members are asked to write or draw pictures of fears that they or others have, one example per paper. They are directed to write as many as they can think of during a five-minute period and to put the completed papers in the glass bottle or jar.

Next, the facilitator puts the lid on the jar and explains that these papers represent fears that someone holds inside of them. The glass jar represents the person holding on to all of these fears. If something bumps the shelf where the jar is stored, it could fall and shatter. If a stressful life experience occurs for someone who is burdened with many held fears, that person can also shatter.

The facilitator then asks for a volunteer to lie on a large piece of butcher paper while another person traces the outline of his or her body. This body form is hung against a flat surface. Group members are asked to choose a color to represent fear and to color in the areas on the large body picture that show where they hold fear. The facilitator asks group members to color lightly if its an area where they feel fear a little and dark where they sense a lot of fear. People may color in the same areas if they have the same sensory experience of the feeling. This picture and the slips of paper with examples of fearful situations are saved for use in upcoming sessions.

Inquiry

The facilitator guides the group sharing of information by adapting the questions and statements in the Activity Inquiry Fan to the content of this experience.

Samples:

How does holding fear inside make someone as fragile as glass?

What were two of the most common places that people held fear in their bodies? What were two of the most common colors used to represent fear? Talk about that.

What kinds of aches and pains do you think people might develop if they continue to hold fear in these places in their body?

Fear on a Scale of 1-10
Practice

Objective
Group members will gain experience handling strong feelings by practicing fear management techniques.

Materials
Slips of paper with writings and drawings about fear from the previous activity, blank slips of paper, pens or pencils, chart paper or white board, markers, tape, two baskets or other containers

Procedure
The facilitator places two baskets in the middle of the table. One basket holds the slips of paper with examples of fear situations on them. The other is empty and will be used later in the activity. The facilitator begins by explaining that people are often told they should not be afraid, or at least should not show that they are afraid—they should be brave. Group members are reminded of how fear that is "bottled up" can cause body aches and pains. People who live in fear do not experience the full range of wonderful human emotions and have difficulty learning new things.

Next, group members are asked to think of some constructive actions that could help them or others manage fear. They write or draw these on blank slips of paper and put them in the empty basket in the middle of the table. The facilitator writes some examples, too, which could include some of the following:
1. Draw a picture of what is frightening you. Put yourself in the picture and draw a protective bubble around yourself.
2. Whistle a happy tune.
3. Talk to someone whom you trust.
4. Carry a wallet card with emergency numbers on it to help you feel secure.
5. Choose to avoid scary books or horror movies.
6. Check around the house at night to see that all of the doors and windows are locked.
5. Find a pretty stone, button, coin, etc., and carry it in your pocket. Rub it when you feel afraid.
6. Move through your day as part of a group, rather than alone.
7. Take a warm bath and have a cup of hot chocolate or tea.

The facilitator asks each group member to take one paper from each basket. One paper will have a frightening event on it, and the other will have an example of a constructive action that could be used to manage fear. The facilitator draws a "Fear Thermometer" such as the one below on chart paper or the white board. On a scale from 0-10 with "0" representing "no fear" and "10" representing "terrified," group members decide how intense their fear would be in relationship to the situation on the paper that they chose. Each in turn tapes the situation papers next to the appropriate number on the "Fear Thermometer."

After people have rated the fear scenarios, they read their constructive action paper and suggest which of the fearful situations it might help manage. If the action doesn't apply to any of them, the group member selects another paper until finding one that is applicable. Group members tape these next to their partner fear paper on the thermometer.

Fear Thermometer

terrified	10
	9
frightened	8
	7
scared	6
	5
afraid	4
	3
worried	2
	1
no fear	0

While discussing the choices that people made, the facilitator points out that when working on fear management it may not be possible to go from "terrified" to "no fear" in one step. Someone who has a lot of "bottled up" fear may want to try to go from a state of feeling "terrified" the majority of the time to feeling "scared" and then to feeling "worried," one step at a time.

Inquiry

The facilitator guides the group sharing of information by adapting the questions and statements in the Activity Inquiry Fan to the content of this experience.

Samples:

How could you apply this information to your daily life?

Would you recommend this activity to another group? Why or why not?

Name three constructive actions that you would choose to use in your life away from group to help you manage fear.

Journal Writing: Managing Fear Checklist
Transfer

Objective

Group members will apply their ability to constructively manage fear to their daily lives.

Materials

Journals, pens or pencils

Procedure

During the upcoming week, the facilitator asks group members to write down times that they are afraid, a constructive action they use to manage the fear, and the outcome.

Overflowing Sorrow
Awareness

Objective

Group members will gain an awareness of the relationship between effectively managing sorrow and their overall well-being as a person.

Materials

A large glass bowl, large drinking glasses full of water (one for each group member and the facilitator), slips of blank paper, pens or pencils, body outline on butcher paper, colored markers, crayons or chalk

Procedure

Group members are asked to use the blank slips of paper to write down experiences they have had that have brought on feelings of sadness, deep sorrow, or grief. Next, the facilitator takes the large bowl, the completed slips of paper, and a glass of water; gives each group member a glass full of water; and leads the group to a private spot outdoors. The bowl is set on the ground and the group forms a circle around it.

Each person is asked to read an example of a sorrowful incident. After each reading, the facilitator asks everyone to pour water into the bowl to show how many tears they might cry in a situation such as the one described. If they would only feel a little sad, they add just a few drops to the bowl. If they would feel deep sorrow, they pour more water into the vessel. If the situation would leave them grief-stricken, they pour a lot of water—perhaps the entire glassful. The facilitator notes that it is okay for the vessel to overflow, because managing the strong feeling of sorrow requires that we be willing to cry or let the feeling wash over us like water. Sorrow and grief can overwhelm a person unless allowed to overflow.

The group returns indoors and turns its attention to the outline of the human body that was created in the previous activity about fear. Now everyone is asked to choose a color to represent sorrow for them. Each group member colors in a part of the body where sorrow is sensed. They color lightly those areas where sorrow is felt just a little and use dark coloring for the areas where it is felt intensely. Group members may color in the same areas if they experience sorrow in the same place as another. The picture and the slips of paper with sad situations written on them are saved for use in upcoming sessions.

Inquiry

The facilitator guides the group sharing of information by adapting the questions and statements in the Activity Inquiry Fan to the content of this experience.

Samples:

Deep sorrow overwhelms the body and has to overflow. What does that mean to you?

Which part of the body held sorrow the most often? Which color represented sorrow most often? Talk about that.

What kinds of aches and pains do you think someone might experience if sorrow is not allowed to overflow?

Sorrow on a Scale from 1-10
Practice

Objective

Group members will gain experience handling strong feelings by practicing sorrow management techniques.

Materials

Slips of paper with writings and drawings about sorrow from the previous activity, blank slips of paper, pens or pencils, chart paper or white board, markers, tape, two baskets or other containers

Procedure

The facilitator places two baskets in the middle of the table. One basket holds the slips of paper with examples of sorrowful situations on them. The other is empty and will be used later in the activity. The facilitator explains that many people have been taught that tears and sadness are a signs of weakness. "Boys don't cry, "Big girls don't cry," or "You crybaby!" are the kinds of statements that make people hide or deny feelings of sadness. Actually, when people are courageous enough to experience and express sadness, they become stronger and more compassionate individuals. Group members are reminded that sorrow signals a time of change and that tears can soothe the sense of loss that accompanies many big changes.

Next, group members are asked to think of some constructive actions that could help them or others manage sorrow. They write or draw these on blank slips of paper and put them in the empty basket in the middle of the table. The facilitator writes some examples, too, and could include some of the following:

1. Draw a picture that depicts sadness. Choose colors that are meaningful to you in the expression of sorrow. Add a small flower somewhere in the drawing to represent hope.
2. Read books about sorrow and grief to learn about how they change over time.
3. Plant a tree or some flowers in memory of something or someone who has gone from you.
4. Sit down and tell a close friend about your sadness. Have a good cry.
5. Write about your sadness as if it were a fairy tale. Begin with, "Once upon a time …." End your story the way you wish your sad experience could end, even if that isn't possible.
6. Exercise by taking a long walk, riding a bike, stretching to music, etc.
7. Take a "beauty walk." Walk and look for as many beautiful things as you can along the way.

The facilitator asks each group member to take one paper from each basket. One paper will have a sad event on it, and the other will have an example of a constructive action that could be used to manage sorrow. The facilitator draws a "Sorrow Thermometer" such as the one on the following page on chart paper or the white board. On a scale from 0-10 with "0" representing "no sorrow" and "10" representing "hopeless," group members decide how intense their sorrow would be in relationship to the situation on the paper that they chose. Each in turn tapes the situation papers next to the appropriate number on the "Sorrow Thermometer."

After people have rated the sorrow scenarios, they read their constructive action paper and suggest which of the sad situations it might help manage. If the action doesn't apply to any of them, the group member selects another paper until finding one that is applicable. Group members tape these next to their partner sorrow paper on the thermometer.

Sorrow Thermometer

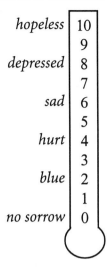

hopeless	10
	9
depressed	8
	7
sad	6
	5
hurt	4
	3
blue	2
	1
no sorrow	0

While discussing the choices that people made, the facilitator points out that when working on sorrow management it may not be possible to go from "hopeless" to "no sorrow" in one step. Someone who is "overflowing" with sorrow may want to try to go from a state of feeling "hopeless" most of the time to feeling "sad" and then to feeling "blue," one step at a time.

Inquiry

The facilitator guides the group sharing of information by adapting the questions and statements in the Activity Inquiry Fan to the content of this experience.

Samples:

How could you apply this information to your daily life?

Would you recommend this activity to another group? Why or why not?

Name three constructive actions that you would choose to use in your life away from group to help you manage sorrow.

Journal Writing: Managing Sorrow Checklist
Transfer

Objective

Group members will apply their ability to constructively manage sorrow in their daily lives.

Materials

Journals, pens or pencils

Procedure

The facilitator asks group members to write down anytime they feel sad during the week, the constructive action they used to manage the sorrow, and what happened next.

Bagging Anger
Awareness

Objective

Group members will gain an awareness of the relationship between effectively managing anger and their overall well-being as a person.

Materials

Medium-sized paper bag, blank slips of paper, body outline on butcher paper, pens or pencils, colored markers, crayons, or chalk

Procedure

The facilitator leads a discussion explaining how anger signals to us that something is happening that we perceive to be harmful to us. The fiery nature of anger requires us to take some kind of action to keep the energy in motion. Group members are asked to use the blank slips of paper and write events that they associate with being angry. They write as many as they can in five minutes and place the papers inside of the bag so that it is stuffed with them.

The facilitator suggests that the slips of paper represent all of the anger that people "stuff" or "bag," rather than manage in an effective manner. The bag represents a person who is full of this "bagged" anger, perhaps because many people have been taught that anger is not a "nice" emotion. The facilitator then blows air into the top of the paper bag until it is taut. The group is asked what it thinks will happen next. The facilitator pops the bags and lets the papers fall out. If anger is not dealt with in productive ways it builds up inside of people until something, probably something minor, causes them to explode in an angry outburst.

The group turns its attention to the body outline already colored with information about fear and sorrow from previous sessions. Group members choose a new color to represent anger and use it to color in the part of the body where they experience anger. People may color in the same areas if they experience anger in the same part(s) of the body as someone else. The facilitator collects the slips of paper about anger and saves them to be used in the next activity.

Inquiry

The facilitator guides the group sharing of information by adapting the questions and statements in the Activity Inquiry Fan to the content of this experience.

Samples:

Some people are described as being "walking time bombs " What do you think that means?

What two parts of the body were chosen most often as being the place where people experience anger? What color *was* chosen most often to represent anger? Why do you think that is?

What kinds of aches and pains do you think someone might develop if anger is not released from the parts of the body where it is experienced?

Anger on a Scale from 1-10
Practice

Objective
Group members will gain experience handling strong feelings by practicing anger management techniques.

Materials
Slips of paper with writings and drawings about anger from the previous activity, blank slips of paper, pens or pencils, chart paper or white board, markers, tape, two baskets or other containers

Procedure
The facilitator places two baskets in the middle of the table. One basket holds the slips of paper with examples of angry situations on them. The other is empty and will be used later in the activity. The facilitator points out to the group that for an action to be a constructive way of managing anger, it must pass the following test:

Does it hurt anyone or anything?
• A "yes" answer means that the action is going to cause the situation to escalate—to get worse.
• A "no" answer means the action has merit as a possible means of managing anger and is worth trying.

Next, group members are asked to think of some constructive actions that could help them or others manage anger. They write or draw these on blank slips of paper and put them in the empty basket in the middle of the table. The facilitator writes some examples, too. These could include some of the following:

1. Choose a color or colors that look "angry" to you, maybe red. Draw or scribble lots of angry pictures.
2. Write about angry feelings in a journal. Any words are OK there, since it's private.
3. Pound on the bed or a pillow. Yell into a pillow or in the shower with the water running.
4. Say over and over, "I am angry because …"
5. Write a letter about your anger and then tear it up and throw it in the air.
6. Walk or run as fast as you can.
7. Bounce a ball hard against a wall and say, "I am mad because …" every time it hits the wall.

The facilitator asks each group member to take one paper from each basket. One paper will have an angry event on it, and the other will have an example of a constructive action that could be used to manage anger. The facilitator draws an "Anger Thermometer"such as the one on the following page on chart paper or the white board. On a scale from 0-10 with "0" representing "no anger" and "10" representing "enraged," group members decide how intense their anger would be in relationship to the situation on the paper that they chose. Each in turn tapes the situation papers next to the appropriate number on the "Anger Thermometer."

After people have rated the anger scenarios, they read their constructive action paper and suggest which of the angry situations it might help manage. If the action doesn't apply to any of them, the group member selects another paper until finding one that is applicable. Group members tape these next to their partner anger paper on the thermometer.

Anger Thermometer

enraged	10
	9
furious	8
	7
mad	6
	5
annoyed	4
	3
grumpy	2
	1
no anger	0

While discussing the choices that people made, the facilitator points out that when working on anger management it may not be possible to go from "enraged" to "no anger" in one step. Someone who has "bagged" a lot of anger may want to try to go from a state of feeling "enraged" all of the time to feeling "mad" and then to feeling "grumpy," one step at a time.

Inquiry

The facilitator guides the group sharing of information by adapting the questions and statements in the Activity Inquiry Fan to the content of this experience.

Samples:
How could you apply this information to your daily life?
Would you recommend this activity to another group? Why or why not?
Name three constructive actions that you would choose to use in your life away from group to help you manage anger.

Journal Writing: Managing Anger Checklist
Transfer

Objective

Group members will apply their ability to constructively manage anger to their daily lives.

Materials

Journals, pens or pencils

Procedure

Group members are asked to write down examples of anger they feel during the upcoming week, constructive actions they take to manage the anger, and the outcome of those actions.

Set III. Purpose:
To provide opportunities for group members to manage strong feelings through effective communication

Strong Feelings: Guidelines and Pitfalls
Awareness

Objective
Group members will gain an awarenesss of guidelines necessary for the effective communication of strong feelings.

Materials
Chart paper or white board, markers

Procedure
The facilitator writes out the "guidelines" side of the chart (below) prior to the group meeting. Group members discuss each guideline and consider its usefulness when communicating strong feelings. Next to each guideline, the facilitator records any potential pitfalls group members think of related to each guideline. Sample pitfalls are noted in parentheses on the chart.

Guidelines for Effective Communication of Strong Feelings	*Pitfalls* (Samples)
1. Focus on behaviors, not people.	1. (attacking a person with words)
2. Use "I" statements, take responsibility for your feelings	2. (blaming someone)
3. Be brief and stay focused on here and now	3. (dredging up the past)
4. Use assertive (not agressive) body language.	4. (trying to communicate when really upset)
5. Allow others to contribute their perspectives.	5. (lambasting others with no regard for their feelings)
6. Consider your motivation.	6. (hurting someone, "paybacks")
7. Consider your expectations.	7. (expecting agreement or apology)
8. Ask if the other person will listen to you.	8. (catching someone off guard, setting yourself up to be rejected)

Inquiry
The facilitator guides the group sharing of information by adapting the questions and statements in the Activity Inquiry Fan to the content of this experience.

Samples:
Describe the two guidelines for the effective communication of strong feelings that are, in your opinion, the most important.

Think of a new title for this activity.

Who are some people with whom you could communicate strong feelings and have a productive outcome?

Communicating Strong Feelings: Format
Practice

Objective

Group members will practice effectively communicating strong feelings by using the Five-Step Assertive Response Model.

Materials

Managing Strong Feelings Role-Play situations (Experiences 12.3 and 12.4)

Procedure

Before group members practice managing strong feelings using the Five-Step Assertive Response Model, the facilitator asks them to revisit the Guidelines for Managing Strong Feelings as discussed in the previous Awareness activity and reiterated in the following questions:

1. Will my intended communication focus on behavior and not people?
2. Am I prepared to take responsibility for my own feelings by using "I" and not "you" statements?
3. Can I be brief and speak only about the present without dredging up past problems?
4. Am I calm enough to be assertive and not aggressive?
5. Can I listen to the other person's point of view as well?
6. What is my motivation for expressing this strong feeling?
7. What do I hope will happen after I express the strong feelings that I have?
8. Is this person someone who will listen to my feelings and ideas?

Next, group members are asked to take turns reading the Managing Strong Feelings Scripts (Experiences 12.3 and 12.4) and completing the Five-Step Assertive Response for each scenario. Several different group members may be asked to do the same role-play situation in order to demonstrate how people handle the same set of circumstances in their own unique manner.

Inquiry

The facilitator guides the group sharing of information by adapting the questions and statements in the Activity Inquiry Fan to the content of this experience.

Samples:

How would you feel if your expectations aren't met? What might you do then?
Name three other ways to manage strong feelings without including anyone else?
Under what circumstances would you choose to not express a strong feeling to another person?

Managing Strong Feelings
Role-Play Situations
Level I

1. Julie was invited to Tara's birthday party. Julie's best friend Amy wasn't invited and she has been avoiding Julie. Julie calls Amy on the phone and says:

    I'd like to talk to you about something that's been bothering me. Can you listen to me now?

    I don't like it when _____.

    I feel _____.

    I want _____.

    I think it would benefit us both if _____.

2. Frank is upset because his classmate, Rob, has been teasing him about his new haircut. Frank goes up to Rob and says:

    I'd like to talk to you about something that's been bothering me. Would you give me a minute?

    I don't like it when _____.

    I feel _____.

    I'd appreciate it if _____.

    I think we both would benefit if _____.

3. Brianna, Valerie, and Jessica have been best friends for two years. Last week Brianna and Valerie began teasing Jessica and leaving her out of their games. Jessica goes up to her friends and says:

    I'd like to talk to you about something that's been bothering me. Can we sit down together for a while?

    I don't like it when _____.

    I feel _____.

    I'd really like it if _____.

    We could all benefit if _____.

4. Kate has three brothers and two sisters. She is upset because her mom never has time to be alone with her. She really wants to talk to her friend about how this feels. She goes up to her friend Michael and says:

    I'd like to talk to you about something that's been bothering me. When would you have time to listen?

    I don't like it when _____.

    I feel _____.

    I want _____.

    I think everyone would benefit if_____.

5. Larry has a vision problem and has to wear thick glasses. In class, Christina giggles at him and calls him "four-eyes." He sees her alone at recess and says:

    I'd like to talk to you about something that's been bothering me. Do you have time to listen?

    I don't like it when _____.

    I feel _____.

    I hope that _____.

    It would benefit us both if _____.

Managing Strong Feelings
Role-Play Situations
Level II

1. Annie was accepted into an overseas summer language institute. Her best friend wasn't chosen and has been avoiding Annie. On the phone, Annie says:

> I'd like to talk to you about something that's been bothering me. Do you have a minute?
> I don't like it when _____.
> I feel _____.
> I want _____.
> It would benefit us both if _____.

2. Karl knows his friend Jim is an alcoholic. He goes to Jim's house and asks him to go for a walk. He says:

> I'd like to talk to you about something that's been bothering me. Is this a good time?
> I don't like it when _____.
> I feel _____.
> I want _____.
> I think it would benefit_____.

3. Jason overhears someone he asked out laughing about him to her friend. He sees her alone and says:

> I'd like to talk to you about something that's been bothering me. Do you have time to listen?
> I don't like it when _____.
> I feel _____.
> I'd appreciate it if _____.
> It would benefit both of us if _____.

4. Jessie is working on a group project with five others. They seem to reject all of her ideas and even seem to be shutting her out of conversations. She asks everyone to stop for a moment and says:

> I'd like to talk to you about something that's been bothering me. Can you all listen to me for a moment?
> I don't like it when _____.
> I feel _____.
> I want _____.
> I think the group would benefit if _____.

5. Bill has grown up with a hearing loss that affects his speech. Mary giggles when he talks in class. He sees her sitting alone at the bus stop and says:

> I'd like to talk to you about something that's been bothering me. May I sit down and tell you about it?
> I don't like it when _____.
> I feel _____.
> I hope _____.
> I think we would both benefit if _____.

Journal Writing: Will You Listen?
Transfer

Objective

Group members will apply their knowledge of the Guidelines for Effective Communication of Strong Feelings and Five-Step Assertive Response Model for communicating strong feelings in real-life situations.

Materials

Journals, paper, pencils

Procedure

Between meetings, group members are asked to utilize the information and skills they have acquired in the previous activities. They are asked to write about events that trigger strong feelings for them during the upcoming week. They are also asked to write or draw what they would say and do if they chose to communicate the strong feelings to the person or people involved. If they do not choose to communicate the strong feelings, they are asked to write or draw what they will do to manage the strong feelings.

Set IV. Purpose:
To provide opportunities for group members to recognize the importance of supportive people in their lives

Stress/Support Scale
Awareness

Objective
Group members will gain an awareness of how much stress and support exists in their lives and how this relates to managing strong feelings.

Materials
Stress and Support Scales (Experiences 12.5 and 12.6)

Procedure
The facilitator distributes the Stress and Support Scales to group members, reviews the directions for how to complete them, and assists with questions that arise. When everyone has completed the scales, participants discuss issues relating to stress and support. "Stress" is defined here as being any factor that causes emotional or physical strain. "Support" refers to people and activities that help sustain someone emotionally and physically. The facilitator points out to the group that an overwhelming amount of stress with little support renders someone unable to cope with day-to-day events. Under such circumstances, people tend to overreact to situations and express strong feelings in unproductive ways.

Inquiry
The facilitator guides the group sharing of information by adapting the questions and statements in the Activity Inquiry Fan to the content of this experience.

Samples:
Describe in your own words how you think strong feelings—fear, sorrow, and anger—are related to stress?
Name two big stresses in your life. Name two of your main support people or activities.
How could you decrease the stress level and increase the level of support in your life?

Stress Scale *

This exercise will help you measure how much stress you have had during the last year. It will also show you how important other people can be in helping you deal with stress. New medical studies show that people who have close friends and family have less mental and physical illness than people who try to go it alone.

Circle each stressful event that happened to you within the last 12 months. Circle the items that are starred (*) only if the event happened more than twice during the year. Add the scores for each item circled and put the total on the line.

Personal

(6) Serious injury or illness
(6) Alcohol, drug, or emotional problem
(4) Death of close friend
(2) * Trouble with friends or neighbors   *Total* _____

Education

(4) Skipped a grade, stayed back a grade, lost a job position, or were promoted at work
(4) Changed schools or jobs
(2) * Trouble with teacher or class subject, trouble with boss or work expectations   *Total* _____

Family

(10) Death of parent or immediate family member
(8) Divorce in family
(6) Separation or reconciliation in family
(6) New stepmother, stepfather, or stepchild
(4) Serious illness or injury of family member
(4) Birth or adoption of sister, brother, or child
(4) New stepbrother or stepsister
(4) Brother, sister, or child leaves home
(4) Relative moves into household
(4) Moved to new house
(4) * Family arguments   *Total* _____

Total Stress Score _____

If Your Stress Level Score is:

Less than 10: You have a low stress level. You have few stressors with which to deal.

10-15: You have a moderate (or medium) stress level. There has been a lot of change in your life.

16 or more: You have a high stress level. There have been major adjustments in your life. This type of stress is
       harmful, especially if it lasts a long time.

_____

* Used with permission from California Department of Mental Health. Adapted from *Mental Health:The Youth Award Handbook*, the Mental Health Association, Los Angeles, California, 1982.

Support Network Scale *

Circle one response for each item. Then add the scores next to each item you circled and put the total in the box.

1. How many persons do you talk to about a school/work problem?
   - (0) none
   - (3) one
   - (4) two or three
   - (5) four or more

   Total _____

2. How many friends do you trade favors with, such as loan items, share meals, help with tasks?
   - (0) none
   - (1) one
   - (2) two or three
   - (3) four or more

   Total _____

3. Do you have a close friend or best friend?
   - (0) no
   - (2) several different friends
   - (6) one steady friend
   - (10) many friends, one best friend

   Total _____

4. How often do friends and close family members visit you at home?
   - (0) rarely
   - (1) about once a month
   - (4) several times a month
   - (8) once a week or more

   Total _____

5. How many friends or family members do you talk to about personal matters?
   - (0) none
   - (6) one or two
   - (8) three to five
   - (10) six or more

   Total _____

6. How often do you participate in a social, community or sports group?
   - (0) rarely
   - (1) about once a month
   - (2) once a week or more

   Total _____

Total Support Scale _____

If Your Suppport Network Score Is:

Less than 10: Your support network has low strength and probably does not provide much support. You need to consider getting closer to people.

15-29: Your support network has moderate strength and likely provides enough support except during periods of high stress.

30 or more: Your support network has high strength, and it will probably maintain your well-being even during periods of high stress.

---

* Used with permission from California Department of Mental Health. Adapted from *Mental Health: The Youth Award Handbook*, the Mental Health Association, Los Angeles, California, 1982.

Circle of Support
More Practice

Objective
Group members will increase the level of support in their lives by identifying current and potential support people.

Materials
"Circle of Support" (Experience 12.7)

Procedure
The facilitator passes out a copy of the "Circle of Support" (Experience 12.7) and asks group members to consider all of the possible levels of support represented in the picture. Next, they are asked to cross out any groups that do not offer support to them. They are then asked to place numbers next to the remaining group names to indicate their level of importance as providers of support, with "1" being the most significant.

Next, the facilitator asks group members to consider the following list of situations and decide with whom they could share the experience using the "Circle of Support" picture as a guide. They are directed to mark the situation letter next to the name of the group on the circle with which they would be comfortable sharing the experience or information.

      A. Laugh really hard with _____.
      B. Tell a big secret to _____.
      C. Get angry with _____.
      D. Cry in front of _____.
      E. Ask for help from _____.
      F. Ask directions from _____.
      G. Ask for money from _____.
      H. Ask for help with solving a problem _____.
      I. Invite home _____.
      J. Tell family problem to _____.

Finally, group members fill in the blanks at the bottom of the "Circle of Support" diagram with the names of specific people who offer them support. They may also add the names of people whom they think would be supportive if asked.

Inquiry
The facilitator guides the group sharing of information by adapting the questions and statements in the Activity Inquiry Fan to the content of this experience.

Samples:
Who do you feel most comfortable with in your "circle of support?"
Do you feel you have enough support? Why or why not?
How could you increase the level of support in your life?

Circle of Support

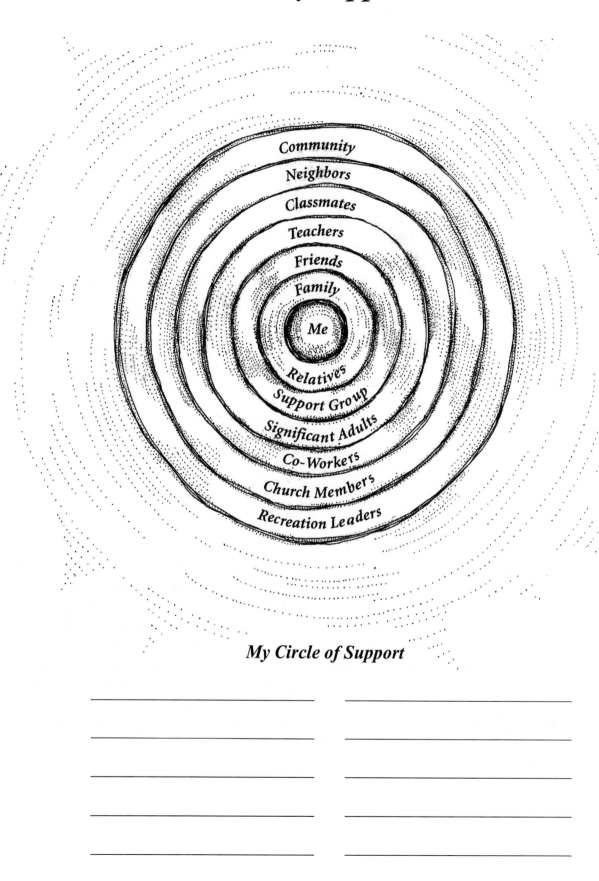

Community
Neighbors
Classmates
Teachers
Friends
Family
Me
Relatives
Support Group
Significant Adults
Co-Workers
Church Members
Recreation Leaders

My Circle of Support

_____   _____

_____   _____

_____   _____

_____   _____

_____   _____

Supportive Friends
Transfer

Objective

Group members apply their knowledge of the need to decrease stress and increase their circle of support in day-to-day living.

Materials

Journals, pens or pencils

Procedure

The facilitator asks group members to write or draw three things that they are going to do in their daily lives to reduce their stress level. Next, they are asked to write about two of the most significant support people in their lives, along with how long they have known this person and how this person has demonstrated support.

To be motivated to resolve conflicts, people must respect themselves, have confidence in their communication skills, and demonstrate comfort with the emotional aspect of being human. These topics were addressed in Chapters 5-7: *Exploring Self, Sharing Ideas,* and *Focusing on Feelings.* The ability to take another person's perspective, to care about the good of the group, to step forward with a point of view, and to listen carefully to the contributions of others are required for successful conflict resolution, as well. These themes were woven through Chapters 8-10. Chapters 11 and 12: *Handling Verbal Abuse* and *Managing Strong Feelings* gave group members tools for dealing with difficult life experiences and intense feelings. When applied, all of these tools lead to the constructive resolution of conflicts and/or keep minor disagreements from escalating into major conflicts. The "challenge factor" of the content from one chapter to the next increased in preparation for the complexity of the final series of activities in *Chapter 13: Resolving Conflicts.*

Facilitator Log

Things to remember:

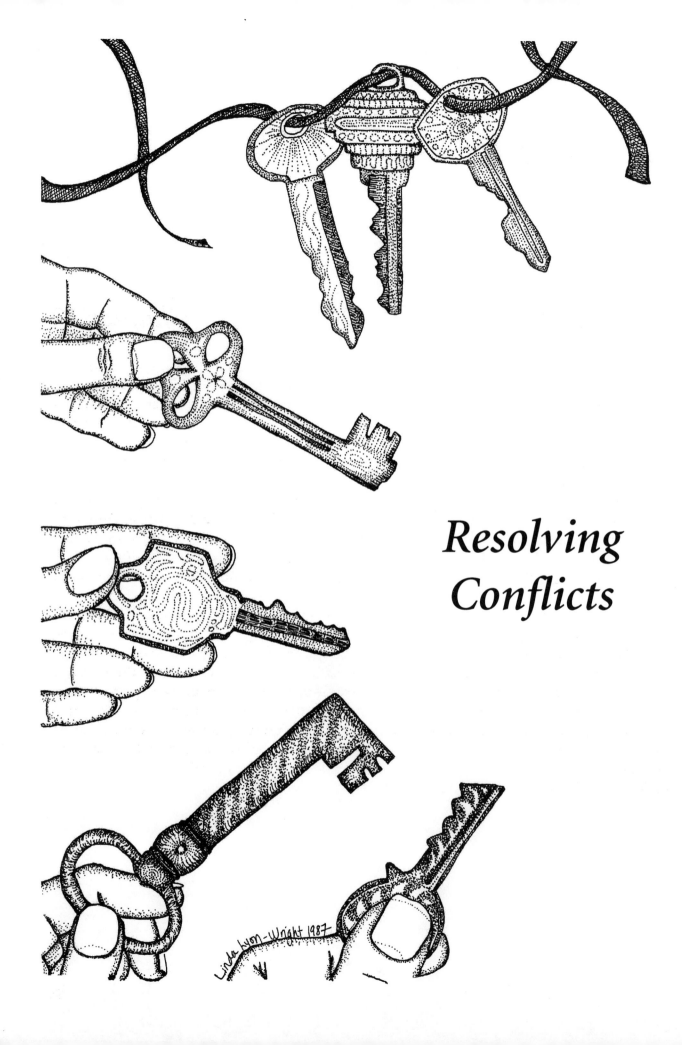

Resolving Conflicts

Linda Lyon-Wright 1987

Chapter 13

Conflict naturally occurs in all types of relationships, whether they are between friends or entire nations of people. Constructive conflict—disputes and disagreements that occur within, between, and among people—fuels creative ideas, leads to personal and collective growth, and ultimately results in the evolution of human thought and action. Conflict that is not addressed and resolved effectively escalates into often violent power struggles, on both a person-to-person and global level.

A key feature of constructive conflict resolution is a belief in "the power of one," the significant effect individual efforts have on the well-being and progress of a much larger group. A tenant of peaceful conflict resolution requires that resolution options be nonviolent. Another critical aspect of effective conflict resolution is adherence to a "win-win" perspective, which means all parties involved in a dispute stop viewing it as a contest and agree to work until everyone is satisfied with a proposed solution. The goal is not to "get rid of" conflict, but rather to discover its creative potential while searching for

mutually agreeable solutions. Finally, people who find meaningful solutions to conflicts are able to do so because they believe that there are at least as many different ways to solve a problem as there are people involved. This celebration of diversity adds vitality to the process.

Group members now have an opportunity to apply the People Skills that they have learned from all previous activities to manifest effective conflict resolution, since an appreciation of self and others, cooperation, clear communication, and emotional expression are all needed to make this happen. The tools that group members learn here will benefit them and others in their lives even more if the significant people in their lives have the same information. A letter that explains the Conflict Resolution Model used in the Belonging Program is provided later in this chapter and is to be shared with families, teachers, and other identified persons as group members become proficient enough with the model to explain it to others.

Set I. Purpose

To provide group members with opportunities to explore the nature of conflict and effective conflict resolution

Conflict in the News
Awareness

Objective

Group members will gain an awareness of the existence of conflict within a person, between people, and among groups of people and nations.

Materials

Current newspaper or weekly magazines that have worldwide news articles

Procedure

The facilitator leads a discussion about different types of conflict—disputes and disagreements that occur within, between, and among people. Group members are asked to think of examples of Internal Conflict, struggles that have gone on inside of them and what they've done to resolve the problem. Next, they are asked to give examples of Conflicts Between People that they have experienced and tell how they were handled. Finally, the group considers Conflict Among Groups of People or Nations and any information that they might have about how these were addressed.

The facilitator then asks group members to go through the newspapers and/or magazines provided and look for articles that illustrate conflict within a person, between two people, or among groups of people or nations. Once everyone has found an article, each person describes the conflict and addresses the following three points:

1. How do the people involved know that a conflict exists?
2. How do you think a resolution could be reached?
3. What could be learned or gained from resolving the conflict?

In a follow-up discussion, the group considers how stagnant the world would be if there was never any conflict. Conflict that is addressed constructively creates a change in circumstance and moves people and events in new directions.

Inquiry

The facilitator guides the group sharing of information by adapting the questions and statements in the Activity Inquiry Fan to the content of this experience.

Samples:

Compare a personal conflict that has been shared with an example of one involving nations from a news publication. How are they the same? How are they different?

What do you think is meant by the statement, "Never underestimate the 'power of one'?" How do the conflicts that you settle with your friends and family relate to the nations of the world?

Name one thing you know about conflict now that you didn't know before today.

Win-Win
Practice

Objective

Group members will practice a cooperative, not competitive, style to become more successful at resolving conflicts.

Materials

None

Procedure

Group members are asked to pair up and sit across from one another with a surface in between them. Each pair chooses to use either right or left hands. The pairs place their elbows on the table in between them and clasp hands. The facilitator then instructs participants to touch the back of their partner's hand on the table as many times as they can in one minute. After the time is up, the facilitator asks how many times their partner's hand touched the table—ten times or more, five-ten times, or zero-five times.

Next, the facilitator describes "win-lose" and "win-win" perspectives on conflict resolution to the group as follows:

In a "win-lose" situation, people come together as competitors. Whatever one person says or does, the other person uses as ammunition to try and overpower the enemy. Tempers flare, people become suspicious of each other, and the conflict gets worse and worse. For one person to be "victorious," the other person must be beaten down until s/he gives in to the first person's point of view. Nothing new is learned and nothing changes. The conflict is still there, only it's buried, waiting to pop out in some other form at a later date.

In a "win-win" situation, people come together cooperatively. All people involved take responsibility for part of the problem, listen to the ideas and needs of others, assert the features of a solution that are important to them, and stand ready to compromise—to give something in order to get something. Both feelings and ideas are respected, people develop trust in one another, and the conflict is resolved. Everyone leaves the conflict feeling satisfied. Bigger problems are avoided when conflicts are resolved at a simpler, personal level.

With this in mind, group members repeat the arm activity. The facilitator reminds them that the goal is to touch their partner's hand to the table as many times as possible.

Inquiry

The facilitator guides the group sharing of information by adapting the questions and statements in the Activity Inquiry Fan to the content of this experience.

Samples:

What did you and your partner do differently the second time that you did the arm activity? Was it more or less successful than the first way you did the activity?

Tell about "win-win" and "win-lose" in your own words.

Make up another way to demonstrate the value of "win-win".

Journal Writing: I Spy Conflict
Transfer

Objective

Group members will apply their knowledge of the nature of conflict and effective conflict resolution to their daily lives.

Materials

None

Procedure

Group members are asked to be private detectives during the week and carefully watch the interactions around them. They are asked particularly to record examples of "win-win" and "win-lose" encounters that they witness. How does it feel to observe a "win-win" versus a "win-lose" situation? Are there more "win-win" or more "win-lose" interactions happening in their daily lives?

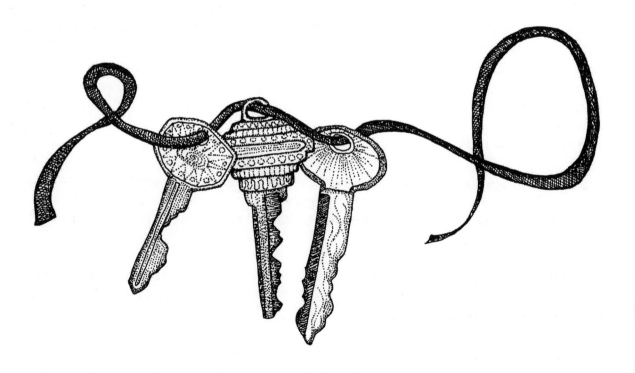

Set II. Purpose:
To provide group members with the knowledge and skill needed to effectively resolve conflicts in their lives

Eight-Step Conflict Resolution Model
Awareness

Objective
Group members will be introduced to an Eight-Step Conflict Resolution Model to gain skills necessary for resolving conflict in their own lives.

Materials
"Eight-Step Conflict Resolution Model" (Experience 13.1), blank sheets of 11x17 drawing paper, colored markers

Procedure
Each group member is given an 11x17 sheet of drawing paper, is instructed to fold it so that there are eight sections, and to number the sections from 1-8, starting in the top left box. The numbers are to be placed in a corner of each square. The facilitator leads the group in a discussion of each step of the "Eight-Step Conflict Resolution Model" and includes the key points noted below. After talking about each step, group members write the title of the step in the appropriately numbered box. Next, they either draw a representation of what happens during that step of the model, or write about it in the box. When completed, these posters are laminated for extended use in the group, at home, or at school.

1. *Calm down.* Those who initiate the problem solving need to carefully "read" their feelings and those of others before attempting to work through the conflict. Are both parties feeling calm and ready to discuss the problem? If not, it's better to wait for a later time.

2. *Ask the Other Person to Listen.* No one can force another person to value cooperation and conflict resolution. If someone isn't willing to work together to resolve a conflict, the other person may want to seek help. Asking also lets the other person know that you have an issue with them so that they aren't taken by surprise.

3. *State the Problem Behavior.* Everyone has an opportunity to express personal thoughts by making an "I don't or didn't like it when …" statement. The focus is on the problem behavior, not on blaming or attacking the other person.

4. *State the Feeling.* All thoughts in a conflict situation are accompanied by feelings. Each person involved has an opportunity to express these by saying something like, "I feel or felt …when …" Using an "I" statement demonstrates that the speaker is taking responsibility for personal feelings and not blaming the other person.

5. *State What You Want or Hope.* Each person has a chance to express wants, hopes, and wishes for a change in the way things are by saying something like, "I want, hope, would appreciate …" In addition, the speaker tells how this would benefit everyone involved by adding a statement such as, "I think we both would benefit …" or "Some of the benefits I see from solving this are …"

6. *Listen to the Other Person.* The most productive way for both sides to be heard is for one person to state the problem behavior, the related feelings, and the wants and benefits without interruption before the second person does the same (Steps 3-5). It is helpful if each speaker restates what they heard the other person say to see if what was intended is what was heard.

7. *Choose Strategies.* After everyone has shared, each begins to suggest creative ways to resolve the conflict. Together they decide upon one to try. They may have one or two ideas as backup for the first one in case it isn't successful. The participants may find it helpful to select a time to check-in with each other to see how well the solution is working.

8. *Seek Help.* Sometimes the best efforts of individuals fail to produce a solution that everyone can support. At such times, the disputants might ask someone they both trust to mediate. They agree on a time to contact the potential mediator to set up a meeting.

Inquiry

The facilitator guides the group sharing of information by adapting the questions and statements in the Activity Inquiry Fan to the content of this experience.

Samples:

Pretend that you're teaching the "Eight-Step Conflict Resolution Model" to your friends. Tell about the eight steps in your own words.

What is the easiest thing about this model? What is the hardest?

Name three people with whom you think you could use this model.

Eight-Step Conflict Resolution Model

1. ***Calm Down.*** Take a walk and breathe deeply. Take a day to think. Listen to music.

2. ***Ask the Person to Listen.*** "I'd really like to talk to you about __________. Will you listen?"

3. ***State the Problem Behavior.*** "I don't like it when __________."

4. ***State the Feeling.*** "I feel __________ when __________."

5. ***State What You Want and the Benefits.*** "I want __________, which I think would benefit us both by __________."

6. ***Listen to the Other Person.*** Both people listen without interruption. Both people restate what they think the other person said to check for understanding.

7. ***Choose a Strategy.*** Have one or two more ideas for backup in case the first fails.

8. ***Seek Help if Needed.*** Contact a trusted person to mediate the conflict.

Linda Lyon-Wright 1987

Conflict Resolution Strategies
Practice

Objective

Group members will practice the "Eight-Step Conflict Resolution Model" while learning effective strategies for resolving conflicts.

Materials

"Eight-Step Conflict Resolution Model" (Experience 13.1), "Conflict Scenes" (Experience 13.2), "Conflict Resolution Strategies" (Experience 13.3), "Resolution Strategy Cards" (Experience 13.4) cut apart into nine separate cards, "Conflict Resolution Letter" (Form 13.5) and copies of the laminated posters made in the previous session

Procedure

Group members begin the session by reviewing the "Eight-Step Conflict Resolution Model," which the facilitator has posted. The "Conflict Scenes" (Experience 13.2) are used to practice the first five steps of the model. Group members volunteer to read the scenarios and fill in the blanks with ideas that they think would lead to a constructive solution.

Next, the facilitator leads a discussion on strategies for resolving conflicts. "Conflict Resolution Strategies" (Experience 13.3) provides the focal point for the conversation about the nine strategies and is posted in the room along with the "Eight-Step Conflict Resolution Model" (Experience 13.1) for ongoing reference.

After the review of the nine suggested strategies for resolving conflicts, the facilitator leads the group in a game using the "Resolution Strategy Cards" (Experience 13.4). The procedure is explained as follows:

1. Someone volunteers to share a real or imaginary conflict.
Example: I saw my friend take a dollar from the desk next to him. Another day, I watched him take a bag of chips from the cafeteria without paying for them.

2. The "Resolution Strategy Cards" are passed out to the remaining group members. Some may get more than one card so that all nine cards are distributed.

3. Each person in turn suggests a way to resolve the problem that was presented to the group using the strategy she or he was dealt, without saying the name of the strategy.
Example: If someone got the "Let it Go" card, the suggestion might be: Tell your friend what you saw, how you felt about it, and what you hope he'll do differently. If he isn't concerned and doesn't want to stop stealing, then you may want to forget about it or forget about the friendship and make new friends.

4. After each suggestion, the rest of the group tries to guess which strategy was being used.

5. Play the game again using other examples of conflict situations.

At the end of this group meeting, group members are given copies of the Conflict Resolution Letter and their laminated "Eight-Step Conflict Resolution Model" posters to take home or wherever else they are to be shared.

Inquiry

The facilitator guides the group sharing of information by adapting the questions and statements in the Activity Inquiry Fan to the content of this experience.

Samples:

Which strategy seems the easiest to use? Which seems the hardest?

Which strategies do you think would be used most often with friends? with family members? among nations?

Pretend that you are teaching your class about resolution strategies. Describe three of the strategies that you like best, using your own words.

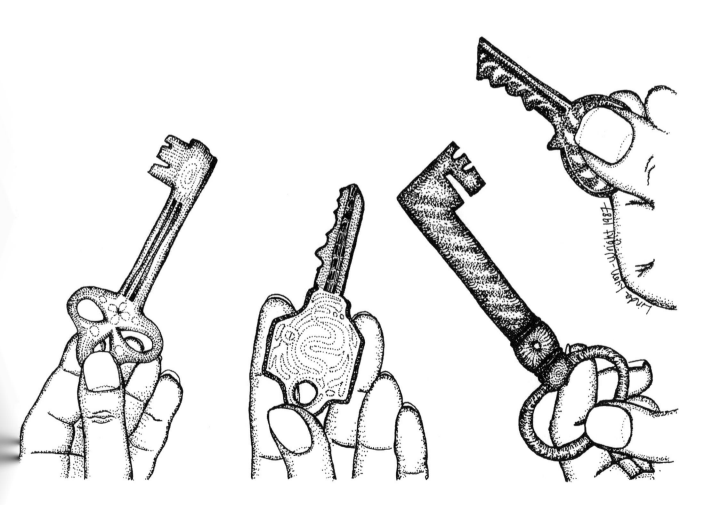

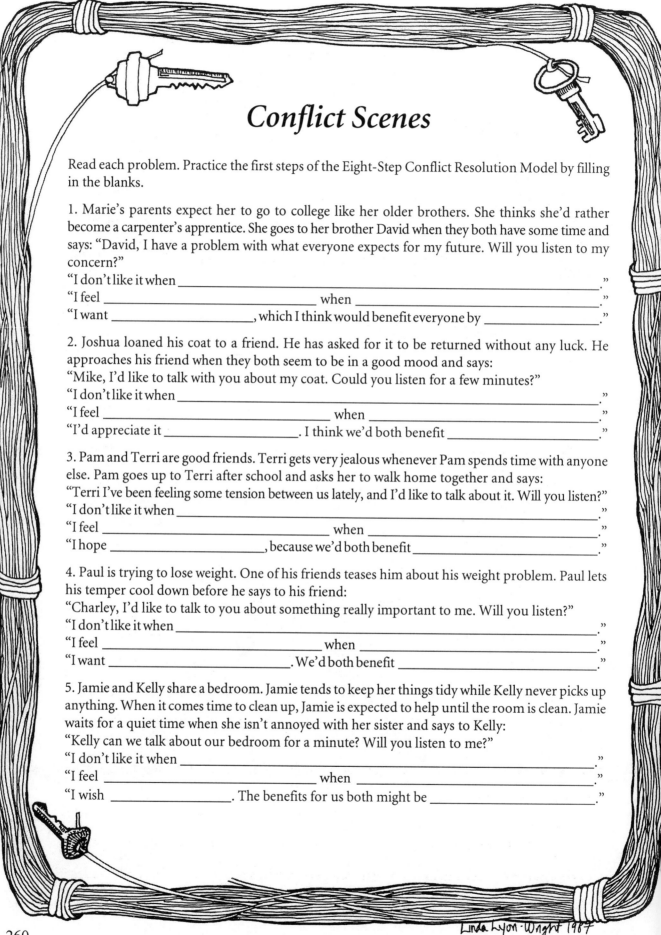

Conflict Scenes

Read each problem. Practice the first steps of the Eight-Step Conflict Resolution Model by filling in the blanks.

1. Marie's parents expect her to go to college like her older brothers. She thinks she'd rather become a carpenter's apprentice. She goes to her brother David when they both have some time and says: "David, I have a problem with what everyone expects for my future. Will you listen to my concern?"

"I don't like it when _____."

"I feel _____ when _____."

"I want _____, which I think would benefit everyone by _____."

2. Joshua loaned his coat to a friend. He has asked for it to be returned without any luck. He approaches his friend when they both seem to be in a good mood and says:

"Mike, I'd like to talk with you about my coat. Could you listen for a few minutes?"

"I don't like it when _____."

"I feel _____ when _____."

"I'd appreciate it _____. I think we'd both benefit _____."

3. Pam and Terri are good friends. Terri gets very jealous whenever Pam spends time with anyone else. Pam goes up to Terri after school and asks her to walk home together and says:

"Terri I've been feeling some tension between us lately, and I'd like to talk about it. Will you listen?"

"I don't like it when _____."

"I feel _____ when _____."

"I hope _____, because we'd both benefit _____."

4. Paul is trying to lose weight. One of his friends teases him about his weight problem. Paul lets his temper cool down before he says to his friend:

"Charley, I'd like to talk to you about something really important to me. Will you listen?"

"I don't like it when _____."

"I feel _____ when _____."

"I want _____. We'd both benefit _____."

5. Jamie and Kelly share a bedroom. Jamie tends to keep her things tidy while Kelly never picks up anything. When it comes time to clean up, Jamie is expected to help until the room is clean. Jamie waits for a quiet time when she isn't annoyed with her sister and says to Kelly:

"Kelly can we talk about our bedroom for a minute? Will you listen to me?"

"I don't like it when _____."

"I feel _____ when _____."

"I wish _____. The benefits for us both might be _____."

Linda Lyon-Wright 1987

Conflict Resolution Strategies

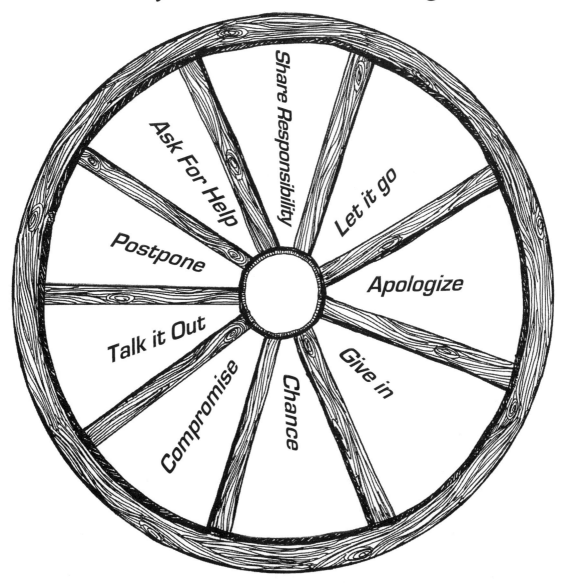

1. *Let it go.* Leave a situation in which resolution probably won't occur.

2. *Apologize.* Say "I'm sorry …," which doesn't necessarily mean that you said or did anything wrong.

3. *Give in.* Decide it's not worth the bother and "give in" to the other person's position.

4. *Chance.* Choose a technique such as flipping a coin or picking a number between 1 and 10 to settle a dispute.

5. *Compromise.* Agree to give up something in order to get something. All involved parties do the same.

6. *Talk it Out.* Keep asking each other questions to gain a better understanding of the different ways people view the same situation.

7. *Postpone.* Agree to wait for a better time to handle the conflict.

8. *Ask For Help.* Seek help from a trusted person when individual efforts have failed.

9. *Share Responsibility.* Admit your contribution to the problem while the other person does the same.

Resolution Strategy Cards

Let it go "If it looks as if you're not getting anywhere, you may want to walk away"	*Apologize* "Have you considered saying you're sorry?" or "Perhaps an apology would work."	*Give in* "If it really doesn't matter much to you, agree to what the other person proposes."
Chance "Why don't you flip a coin?" or "How about drawing straws?" or "You could pick a number between 1 and 10."	*Compromise* "Maybe both of you could give up something in order to get something and settle the dispute."	*Talk it out* "Maybe if you keep asking each other questions, you might understand each other's point of view better."
Postpone "Perhaps it would be better to talk about this problem at another time."	*Ask For Help* "You might consider getting someone else to help you."	*Share Responsibility* "Maybe each of you can figure out what is your share of the problem and agree to work on it."

Conflict Resolution Letter

Dear Parents/Guardians, Teachers, and Friends,

We have been working together to learn effective ways to resolve conflicts that occur among people. We each created a poster to hang up at home and other important places which illustrates the Eight-Step Conflict Resolution Model that we use and which is presented for you here.

1. Calm Down. Make sure that you've "cooled off" enough to work on the conflict.

2. Ask the Other Person to Listen. "I have a concern. Will you listen to me?"

3. State the Problem. "I don't/didn't like it when …"

4. Tell How You Feel. "I felt …when …"

5. Tell What You Want. "I'd appreciate it if …" or "I want …" or "I hope …"

6. Listen to the Other Person. Show respect for the other person by listening to his or her point of view. Restate what the other person said to check for understanding.

7. Choose a Strategy. Choose a way to resolve the conflict and try it out. Talk about other ideas, too, in case the first one doesn't work. Agree to meet again to see if it's working. A list of Strategies for Resolving Conflict is attached.

8. Seek Help. Think of people you could go to for help if you cannot resolve the conflict alone. Agree on a time to contact them.

We have been practicing this model and using it with friends. We've also learned about asking for help if the conflict involves physical aggression or if our individual efforts aren't successful.

We hope that you will try out our model and strategies for resolving conflict, too. Ask us questions. Let us show you what we know how to do!

Thank You!

Members of _____ Support Group

Journal Writing: My Fairy Tale
Transfer

Objective

Group members will apply their knowledge of conflict resolution strategies to an imaginary conflict situation.

Materials

Paper or journal, pens, pencils

Procedure

During the upcoming week, group members are asked to write an original fairy tale complete with a hero/heroine, a villain, and a big problem. Unlike most fairy tales, however, the conflict in this one is to be resolved in a "win-win" manner, using the conflict resolution strategies.

Set III. Purpose:

To provide group members with a mediation format for resolving conflicts with assistance

Mediation
Awareness

Objective

Group members will gain an awareness of (1) breakdowns that occur when trying to resolve a conflict and (2) the value of seeking help through mediation.

Materials

"Resolution Checklist" (Experience 13.6), pencils or pens

Procedure

The facilitator leads a discussion about the value of seeking help when two or more parties are unable to settle a dispute and emotions become heated. A mediator is a neutral person who is willing to stand in between two disputing parties and help them reconcile their differences. Resolutions can be reached and people can move out of seemingly hopeless stalemates as long as the disputants remain willing to communicate and the mediator is skilled and patient. The discussion then focuses upon why individual efforts fail. Among the most common reasons are: (1) breakdowns in communication, (2) never really getting to the heart of the problem, and (3) the choice of unrealistic solutions.

Breakdowns in Communication. Many breakdowns in communication occur because someone's viewpoint was misunderstood or misconstrued. Restating or paraphrasing what someone else says is the most effective way of avoiding this and of telling someone that they are really being taken seriously. This point can be emphasized in the following short activity:

The facilitator introduces a discussion topic in one sentence. For example, "I really have a hard time watching the news these days. There is so much violence in the world." The next person adds to the discussion only after paraphrasing what the previous person said. For example, "You are upset by the violence in world news and don't like to watch news broadcasts for that reason. I don't like to watch them either. I like to focus on things I can make better in the world around me." The following person paraphrases the remarks of the preceding speaker and then adds new ideas. For example, "You take an interest in solving the problems in your own life. I do, too, but I also make donations to world organizations that promote the well-being of people who live in dire straits." The process of paraphrasing and adding to the conversation continues around the circle. Group members are encouraged to ask if what they said represented the speaker's intention.

Never Getting to the Heart of the Problem. Many conflicts have underlying issues that aren't as apparent as those on the surface. The facilitator asks the group to listen to one of the following two scenarios to determine the real reason for the conflict.

Level 1
Carrie was mortified because she showed up at Sarah's birthday slumber party a day early on Friday instead of Saturday. At school on Monday, she saw Sarah and some of the other girls whispering to a group of boys. She was sure that they were talking about her. After school Sarah asked Carrie if she wanted a ride home, and Carrie pretended that she didn't hear her.

Level 2
Jim told the other members of the band that Ryan was on probation for shoplifting sound equipment from the mall last year in the community where he used to live. Ryan had not wanted anyone to know about that. He was trying to make a fresh start. The next time the band practiced, Jim laughed when Ryan played off-key. Ryan quit the band and stormed out.

Unrealistic Solutions. Sometimes in eagerness to resolve a conflict, the disputants come up with solutions that cannot be carried out, or when carried out are not fair to both parties. The conflict is renewed, perhaps with more intensity. The facilitator asks group members to use the Resolution Checklist (Experience 13.6) to determine if a proposed solution is realistic.

Inquiry

The facilitator guides the group sharing of information by adapting the questions and statements in the Activity Inquiry Fan to the content of this experience.

Samples:
Describe three main reasons why conflict resolution attempts fail and ways to avoid them.
Act out the "Eight-Step Conflict Resolution Model" and choose a strategy to resolve the underlying conflict in the "Getting to the Heart of the Problem" section.
Use the "Resolution Checklist" to determine if the resolution that you came up with is realistic or not.

Resolution Checklist

This is the solution that we are going to try:

_____

_____

_____.

Yes   No

( )   ( )   1. Does everyone have an equal amount to do to solve the problem?

( )   ( )   2. Can people really do what they said they would?

( )   ( )   3. Will the resolution really solve the problem?

( )   ( )   4. Is the resolution clear and detailed enough ? (Does it provide information about who will do what, when, where, and how much, for how long,etc.)

Linda Lyon-Wright 1987

Mediation
Practice

Objective

Group members will practice mediation techniques to add another dimension to their conflict resolution skills.

Materials

"Mediation Model" (Experience 13.7), "Conflict Resolution Strategies" (Experience 13.3), "Resolution Checklist" (Experience 13.6), "Conflict Scenes" (Experience 13.2)

Procedure

The facilitator leads a discussion of the "Mediation Model," which works well with one to three individuals, or groups of individuals when one person acts as spokesperson for each group. The following are the important features of that discussion:

1. *Agree to Ground Rules.* The mediator asks each participant to state the ground rules aloud.
   I agree to:
   • Listen without interrupting
   • Be respectful, even when I disagree or am feeling upset
   • Tell the truth
   • Work until we resolve the conflict

2. *Calm Down.* The mediator makes sure that all parties are calm and ready to work on the problem together. If not, the mediator asks the participants to do some relaxation exercises, such as deep breathing, stretching, or walking together with the mediator.

3. *Decide Who Goes First.* The mediator asks if anyone would like to go first. If no one does or both people do, the facilitator tosses a coin, or finds another fair way to decide.

4. *First Speaker Shares.* The mediator guides the first person to share his or her version of the conflict using an "I" statement format.
   "I didn't like it when …," "I felt …when …," "I hope that …," "I think this would benefit …"

5. *Restate What Was Said.* The mediator paraphrases what the first speaker said and asks if that is what was intended.

6. *Second Speaker Shares.* The mediator guides the second person to share his or her version of the conflict using an "I" statement format.
   "I don't like it when …," "I feel …when …," "I want …, which would benefit us both …"

7. *Restate What Was Said.* The mediator paraphrases what the second speaker said and asks if that was what was intended.

8. *Summarize the Problem.* The mediator clearly states the problem, combining the information given by both parties, and asks if there are any underlying problems or other resentments that haven't been dealt with that are now contributing to this conflict. If so, Steps 4-8 are repeated until all related problems have been clarified.

9. *Brainstorm Resolutions.* The mediator records all suggested resolutions on chart paper. The "Conflict Resolution Strategies" (Experience 13.3) are used to stimulate ideas.

10. *Choose a Resolution.* The mediator assists in the selection of two or three resolution strategies,which are then circled on the brainstorming chart. The "Resolution Checklist" (Experience 13.6) is applied to these to determine if they are realistic. One is chosen to implement. The participants sign their names next to the chosen strategy on the chart, which is then rolled up and kept by the mediator until the follow-up meeting.

11. *Report Back.* The mediator sets a time for everyone to meet again, which holds people accountable for carrying out their part of the agreement. Also, there is security in knowing that someone is waiting to be supportive, no matter what the outcome of this first attempt.

Once this model is understood, group members practice using it with conflicts from their own lives or use those in "Conflict Scenes" (Experience 13.2). At first the facilitator serves as the mediator, and then group members volunteer for the position. The "Mediation Model" (Experience 13.7) and "Conflict Resolution Strategies" (Experience 13.3) are posted to serve as guides for this role-playing.

Inquiry

The facilitator guides the group sharing of information by adapting the questions and statements in the Activity Inquiry Fan to the content of this experience.

Samples:

Name two benefits of working with a mediator.

What do you think might happen if people cannot resolve a conflict alone and won't agree to mediation?

What are the easiest parts of the mediation process? What are the hardest?

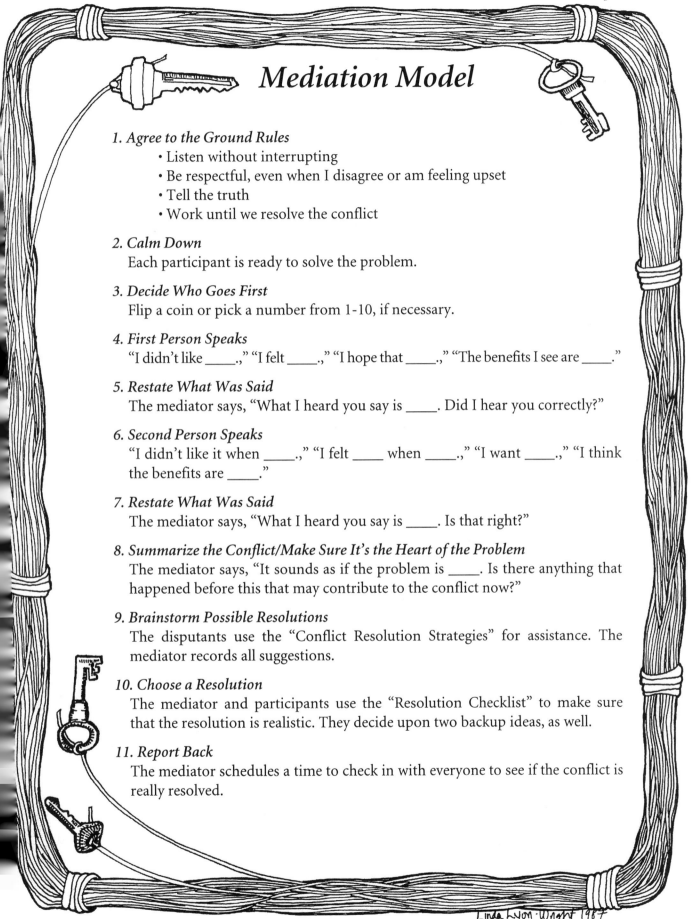

Mediation Model

1. Agree to the Ground Rules
- Listen without interrupting
- Be respectful, even when I disagree or am feeling upset
- Tell the truth
- Work until we resolve the conflict

2. Calm Down
Each participant is ready to solve the problem.

3. Decide Who Goes First
Flip a coin or pick a number from 1-10, if necessary.

4. First Person Speaks
"I didn't like ____.," "I felt ____.," "I hope that ____.," "The benefits I see are ____."

5. Restate What Was Said
The mediator says, "What I heard you say is ____. Did I hear you correctly?"

6. Second Person Speaks
"I didn't like it when ____.," "I felt ____ when ____.," "I want ____.," "I think the benefits are ____."

7. Restate What Was Said
The mediator says, "What I heard you say is ____. Is that right?"

8. Summarize the Conflict/Make Sure It's the Heart of the Problem
The mediator says, "It sounds as if the problem is ____. Is there anything that happened before this that may contribute to the conflict now?"

9. Brainstorm Possible Resolutions
The disputants use the "Conflict Resolution Strategies" for assistance. The mediator records all suggestions.

10. Choose a Resolution
The mediator and participants use the "Resolution Checklist" to make sure that the resolution is realistic. They decide upon two backup ideas, as well.

11. Report Back
The mediator schedules a time to check in with everyone to see if the conflict is really resolved.

Linda Lyon-Wright 1987

Journal Writing: Imaginary Mediation
Transfer

Objective
Group members will apply their mediation skills to a real-life or imaginary conflict.

Materials
Journal, pencils, markers, "Mediation Model" (Experience 13.7)

Procedure
During the upcoming week, the facilitator asks group members to think of a time two friends or two groups of friends were arguing. They are asked to imagine that they are a neutral party who has been asked to mediate the situation. They then draw the scene and use the "Mediation Model" (Experience 13.7) to tell how the conflict was resolved, step-by-step.

Set IV. Purpose:
To provide opportunities for group members to value diverse natures and life experiences as they relate to conflict resolution

Many Faces, Many Masks
Awareness

Objective
Group members will gain an awareness of the diversity that exists in the group.

Materials
Paper plates, glue or glue gun and glue sticks (supervised), tape, felt pens, paint, yarn, pipe cleaners, raffia, buttons, ribbon, colored construction paper, glitter, sequins, etc.
Variations: Fimo clay, plasticine clay, 2" plaster wrap from a medical supply store, Vaseline, old shirts

Procedure
The group facilitator explains that the end-product of this mask-making activity is to be a mask that represents the unique qualities of each individual, those things that make them different from the person next to them. The facilitator then demonstrates how a paper plate can be used as the base for creating a mask. Eyes and other facial features are drawn or cut out with eyebrows added to show emotion. Hair is made to be curly or straight, long or short, with yarn, ribbon, raffia, or pipe cleaners. Group members are encouraged to be creative with their projects.

Variation 1: Two-sided Masks

Group members are asked to create a two-sided mask using paper plates and the Materials described above. On one side, they show how they express themselves to others—their public self. On the other side, they show what is going on inside of them—the private self.

Variation 2: Clay Masks

The facilitator provides Fimo or plasticine clay for group members to use when creating their masks. The clay comes in a variety of colors and air dries. It is made into masks by kneading and manipulating the clay. Group members make their masks three-dimensional by adding clay pieces for eyes, eyebrows, nose, mouth, and hair. This mask-making project requires several sessions to complete.

Variation 3: Plaster Wrap Masks

The facilitator explains that these masks are a lot of fun to make but the process is very messy and requires trust. Group members are asked to find a compatible partner.

The facilitator passes out a roll of 2"-wide plaster wrap for use by each pair of people. Group members are instructed to cut the entire roll of plaster wrap into two to three inch strips.

The process begins after the pair decides who will go first. The first person sits in a chair and covers his or her clothing with an old shirt to protect it from plaster drips. The other partner carefully spreads a thin layer of Vaseline on the face of the person whose mask is being made. It's important to put Vaseline on the eyebrows and any other facial hair to keep the plaster from sticking to the face. Members need to decide if they want their eyes open or closed. The mask can be made around the eye area, leaving a hole for the person's eyes, or the eyes can be completely covered by the plaster wrap.

Next, the plaster strips are dipped in water and gently placed on the Vaseline-covered face. Group members are guided to start on the forehead and work toward the chin with each piece overlapping the last. For a strong mask, group members need to apply two layers. After the mask completely covers the face, the seated person is instructed to remain still for 3-5 minutes for the plaster to "set." When it has hardened, the partner gently lifts it off the seated person's face. The masks are set aside to dry and are decorated the following week.

The process is repeated for the other person. One advantage of this type of mask is that it conforms to the facial structure, which makes it a very personal representation of a group member.

Inquiry

The facilitator guides the group sharing of information by adapting the questions and statements in the Activity Inquiry Fan to the content of this experience.

Samples:

How did it feel to create a mask?

What does your mask say about you? What do others' masks tell about them?

How do you think our diversity relates to the way that we handle conflict?

Walk in My Shoes
Practice

Objective

Group members will gain knowledge of the diverse natures and experiences of people in the group and how these factors effect the way each person relates to conflict situations.

Materials

"Walk In My Shoes Survey" (Experience 13.8), pens or pencils

Procedure

The facilitator leads a discussion about how our individual natures and life experiences influence the way that we interact with the world. People possess unique qualities that seem to be theirs from birth. And their perceptions have been effected by the events that have transpired in their lifetime. These two factors, sometimes called "nature and nurture," effect the way that individuals deal with conflict. Something that bothers one person because of a past experience has no effect upon another. Actions that upset one person may "roll off" another person who is less sensitive and more action-oriented, for example.

Group members are given copies of the "Walk in My Shoes Survey" (Experience 13.8) and are asked to complete them without consulting anyone else. After everyone is finished, each person shares the answer chosen for each item. Group members discuss what that says about the diversity in the group in terms of who might "think," "feel," "act," or "consider others" most often by nature.

Inquiry

The facilitator guides the group sharing of information by adapting the questions and statements in the Activity Inquiry Fan to the content of this experience.

Samples:

What do you think "nature and nurture" means?

List two examples of how people initially react to conflict differently because of "nature and nurture."

What did you learn about group members that you didn't know before?

Walk in My Shoes
Part I

For each item, circle the letter of the first thing that you would probably do in that situation from the choices given. There are no right or wrong answers.

1. You join a community effort to do clean-up jobs for elderly people in the community. You:
    a. spend part of the day getting to know the people you are helping.
    b. come with a plan for how to get the job done efficiently.
    c. make a game out of the tedious chores and race with another person to see who gets done faster.
    d. go home and write in your journal about how good it felt to help someone else.

2. You are told that you were selected to go to Italy on a study trip this summer. You:
    a. run two miles to your friend's house to tell her the news.
    b. start making a list of things to take.
    c. sit in stunned silence before sharing the news with your family.
    d. call the program office to see who will be traveling with you.

3. You are assigned to a group to complete a school project. You:
    a. start pulling everybody's desks together to get going.
    b. offer to be the recorder to organize everyone's contribution.
    c. worry that people aren't going to do their share of the work load.
    d. start to define the task and all of the parts that have to be completed.

4. You find a lost puppy. You:
    a. call Animal Regulation and inform them of your find.
    b. try to figure out where it may have come from by checking with neighbors.
    c. sit and pet it for a long time to soothe its fear.
    d. take it to the park and play with it.

5. You're home alone at night and the electricity goes out. You:
    a. get very frightened and start to cry.
    b. call the neighbors to see if you can go to their house.
    c. phone the electric company to see the nature of the problem.
    d. run done the block to see how many houses have lights out.

6. You come home from school and are told that your grandma died. You:
    a. hug your mom and tell her how sorry you are.
    b. ask how and when she died.
    c. start making a sympathy card for your grandpa.
    d. feel angry and wonder why it had to be your grandma.

Linda Lyon-Wright 1987

Walk in My Shoes

Part II

I. Read each of the life stories presented below.

    A. Marie is 10 years old. She was born in the inner city and has always lived in a big apartment complex. Her mom has raised her and her three brothers alone. She's had to work hard to make ends meet.

    B. Svetlana came to the United States from Russia when she was seven years old. She was an orphan who came to live in a small family in a little beach community. She didn't know how to speak English and felt very afraid.

    C. Joshua is twelve years old and has been raised in an alcoholic family. He's had a lock on his bedroom door for years so that he can hide from the arguments that frequently occur. He relies on his friends and their parents for support.

    D. Jose and Miguel are identical twins who live in an upper-class neighborhood in the suburbs. Both of their parents are professionals. The boys go to a private school, have lot of possessions, have great clothes and have had many opportunities to travel in their 15 years of life.

II. Now read the following potential conflict and decide how each person described above might react to it. Explain.

    1. Someone shows up at school wearing your favorite jacket which has been missing for a few days. You:
        a. go up to the person and threaten to sue them for stealing your property.
        b. go up to them, look them in the eye, and tell them to give back the jacket that your mom gave you for Christmas.
        c. go to your room when you get home and cry because you lost something.
        d. go to your friend's house and ask for advice, because you're afraid the person will yell at you if you ask for the jacket back.

    2. A friend turns pale and asks to be excused from class and doesn't return. You:
        a. feel sick inside and cannot concentrate because you are so worried.
        b. go up to the teacher and ask for a pass to go check on your friend.
        c. run out of class after them and help them to the office.
        d. spend the rest of class writing your friend a note of support.

    3. You go to the movies with a friend, and the people behind you talk and laugh and constantly interrupt the movie. You:
        a. hope somebody else tells them to be quiet.
        b. turn around and tell them to shut up!
        c. whisper to your friend that you want to move to another row.
        d. turn around and politely ask them to stop talking so that you can hear the movie.

Linda Lyon-Wright 1987

Journal Writing: Nature and Nurture
Transfer

Objective

Group members will apply their knowledge of how diverse natures and life experiences effect the way that people perceive and initially react to conflict.

Materials

Journals, pencils or pens

Procedure

Group members are asked to reflect upon their own nature and life experiences during the upcoming week. They are asked to write down any conflict situations that arise and how their initial reactions tell about who they are as a person and what they have experienced so far in life.

Everything about human interactions is an ongoing process of growth and change. As soon as we think of one more concept to explore, others spring from that one. We could continue this journey ad infinitum but decided to stop here. We figure that anyone who masters these skills and cares enough about the health of our world to use them is more than ready to tackle the challenges of the new millennium. So ends our gift to the next generation ... for now.

Facilitator Log

Things to remember:

_____

_____

_____

_____

_____

_____

_____

_____

_____

_____

_____

_____

_____

_____

_____

_____

_____

_____

_____

_____

_____

Bibliography

Cooper, JoAnn. *Handling Anger: A Program for Second to Fourth Grade Students*. Warminster, PA: Marco Products, Inc., 1994.

Foster-Harris, Elizabeth S. *More Energizers and Icebreakers Book II*. Minneapolis, MN: Educational Media Corporation, 1994.

Friedman, Alice and Fran Schmidt. *Creative Conflict Solving for Kids*. Miami Beach, FL: Grace Contrino Abrams Peace Education Foundation, 1985.

Gibbs, Jeanne. *Tribes: A New Way of Learning Together*. Santa Rosa, CA: Center Source Publications, 1994.

Halligan, Jim, Meg Holmberg, and Gail Sadalla. *Conflict Resolution: An Elementary School Curriculum*. San Francisco, CA: The Community Board Program, 1990.

Karns, Michelle. *How to Create Positive Relationships with Students: A Handbook of Group Activities and Teaching Strategies*. Champaign, IL: Research Press, 1994.

Kreidler, William J. *Teaching Conflict Resolution Through Children's Literature*. New York: Scholastic Professional Books, 1994.

Lott, Lynn and Jane Nelsen. *Positive Discipline in the Classroom*. Orem, UT: Empowering People, 1997.

Pudney, Warwick and Eliane Whitehouse. *A Volcano in My Tummy: Helping Children to Handle Anger*. Gabriola Island, BC, Canada: New Society Publishers, 1996.

Index

A

Order Form

Quantity	Item	Unit Price	Total

Subtotal

California residents add 7.25% Sales Tax

Shipping & Handling ($3 for 1st item; $1 each additional)

TOTAL

Name:

Address:

Zip:

Phone:

For faster service, use your credit card and our
toll-free 24-hour order line:
1-888-201-2501
Or, fax your order: 1-805-543-1085
E-mail: sovtypress@thegrid.net
General Information: 1-805-543-6100

Method of Payment

☐ Check enclosed ☐ VISA ☐ Master Card ☐ Discover Card

Account # _____ Exp: _____

Authorizing Signature:

Daytime Phone:

Mail you order with a check or money order made
payable to:
Sovereignty Press
1241 Johnson Ave., #353
San Luis Obispo, CA 93401

Allow 2-3 weeks for delivery. Prices subject to change.

Belonging:
Self and Social Discovery for
Children and Adolescents
$24.95

Belonging Posters

**Perfect companions to
The Belonging Group Process!**

People who have worked with The Belonging Group Process have identified a need for certain aspects of the program to be posted on the wall for constant referral by group members. In response to this need, we have developed the following 22x34 inch posters:

#1 - Alphabet of Emotions Poster
(Experience 7.1)

#2 - Group Process Poster
*Group Process (Form 3.1) and
Group Agreements (Form 3.3)*

#3 - Conflict Resolution Poster
*Conflict Resolution Strategies (Experience 13.3) and
The Eight-Step Conflict Resolution Model
(Experience 13.1)*

$10.95 each

#4 - Order set of 3 posters for
$29.95

Other titles available from Sovereignty Press:

*The Nurses' Career Guide:
Discovering New Horizons in Health Care
$23.95*

*The Companion Workbook
$12.95
The Instructor's Manual
$17.95*

SOVEREIGNTY
P R E S S